— Real Food —
recipes for your
Breadmaker

— Real Food —
recipes for your
Breadmaker

Carol Palmer

foulsham
LONDON • NEW YORK • TORONTO • SYDNEY

foulsham

The Publishing House, Bennetts Close, Cippenham,
Slough, Berkshire, SL1 5AP, England

*To my husband Phil and my children, Emma and Joe, who have
nearly burst with the amount of bread they have consumed in
trying out these recipes!*

ISBN 0-572-02771-0

Printed in Great Britain by Cox & Wyman Ltd, Reading, Berks

Contents

Introduction

The ploy of brewing fresh coffee or baking bread has long been used as a 'welcoming' smell in the home environment. A good idea in theory, but anyone who has ever made their own bread will know that it can be a long drawn-out process that is not always justified by the end results. Cooking a successful loaf can be a rather hit-and-miss affair. There are a number of very important factors that govern the results and we don't all have the time or the energy to spend on something that we can quite easily buy in the supermarket. However, nothing compares to the flavour of home-made bread and now it is possible for even the most inexperienced of cooks to bake their own bread successfully using a breadmaker.

There is a wide range of breadmaking machines now available, which offer a variety of cycles and functions to make breadmaking a pleasure rather than a chore. I have been baking bread by the traditional method for about 20 years, but I am more than impressed with the results I have had from the range of breadmakers I have tested. To get the maximum benefit from this appliance, however, you will probably want to explore beyond the realms of a basic loaf of white bread and this book will help you do just that. Whether you have a penchant for continental-style bread or prefer the traditional bakery favourites, there will be something here for you to try.

Once you have made some of the basic recipes, be bold and try something a little different. None of the recipes is complicated because the breadmaker itself is a simple machine. Eventually, you will feel brave enough to develop your own recipes. But don't think that breadmakers, and indeed this book, are just for special occasions: once you get into the routine of using the machine, you will find that it is a useful tool for every day, whether making sandwiches for the kids or bread for a special buffet.

If you are completely new to the breadmaker, then initially take some time to examine your machine and read the manufacturer's instruction manual. Once you have done this, start by following one of the basic recipes in this book such as white or brown bread. You may need to adjust quantities slightly to suit your particular machine. If you are happy with the results you achieve, then the world is your oyster! Try other recipes in the book and discover your favourites before you move on to experimenting with your own creations. Follow the guidelines for use carefully and take time to read the introductory passages of this book before you embark on your first cooking adventure. But, whatever you do, have fun!

About your breadmaker

*I*t is difficult to generalise about your breadmaker as there is now such a wide range of models available on the market. To mention just a few, there are those that bake two small loaves, compact models for your work surface and those that cook a long, large loaf. To complicate matters, many of the instruction manuals recommend slightly different procedures. However, whatever your model, many of the basic features and principles are the same.

It is probably fair to say that they all consist of a removable non-stick bread pan, which is heated by an electric element housed at the base of the machine. Within the bread pan are either one or two paddles/blades, which rotate during mixing and kneading. The hot 'oven' atmosphere results from the lid, which is closed when the machine is working.

Settings and functions

All the breadmakers I have tested and encountered include such basic programmes as BASIC, WHOLEMEAL/WHEAT and DOUGH. Most now also have FRENCH/CONTINENTAL/ SPECIALITY, JAM and CAKE options. Some offer a vast range of other more elaborate choices. To use the vast majority of recipes in this book, it is necessary to have only the basic range of programmes and, as your confidence grows in using your machine, you will enjoy experimenting with different programmes and recipes. However, as a rule of thumb, if you are unsure always use the BASIC cycle. (See the notes on page 13 for choice of cycle.)

Most breadmakers give you a colour crust option so that you can choose the appearance of your final loaf. Some also offer EXTRA BAKE and KEEP WARM functions. The first is useful if your bread is noticeably pale or wet when you go to remove it. The second is used to keep bread warm if that's how you want to eat it. Many loaves taste better warm, but remember that it does affect their cutting quality.

Most of the machines display the cycle you have selected and the time it will take. Generally, they also have a buzzer or beeper that sounds after the first kneading to signify when to add ingredients such as raisins and nuts that you do not wish to become minced up.

The timer option, present on the majority of breadmakers, allows you to delay the time the cycle commences. It is important that you calculate the time that you want the bread to be ready and delay the time until then, rather than the time you want it to start. Your instruction manual will explain how you set this.

The bread pan and paddles

Some bread pans are quite heavy, others relatively lightweight, though the results are not noticeably different. A handle allows you to lift the pan out of the machine to insert the paddles and put in the ingredients. It is essential that you always do this and do not attempt to add ingredients while the pan is still in the machine – if anything gets down the side of the pan, it will cause burning when the machine is switched on and could damage the element. Once the ingredients are in the pan, it can simply be pushed back down into position. Check that it has locked into position or the machine will fail to operate. Similarly, ensure that the paddle or paddles are firmly engaged before you put the ingredients in the pan. It is very difficult to adjust them once the food is in there, and NEVER attempt to adjust them once the machine is switched on, even if they are not turning.

Always wait until the pan and paddles have cooled down before you attempt to clean them. Never use metal or anything abrasive against the pan or paddles as the surface can easily be damaged and bread will then stick to it. Use warm soapy water and a dishcloth, sponge or soft brush to clean the inside. The paddles can be immersed in water, but not the pan. Fill it with water but never place its underside in water – only the inside should require cleaning. In some cases you may simply be able to wipe it out with a cloth but, if it is very dirty or the paddles seem stuck, allow the inside to soak for a little while.

Normal household washing-up liquid is all that is needed; never use strong cleaners or chemicals.

Safety tips

These are common sense, but important enough to mention here:

◇ Never plug in or operate the machine with wet hands.
◇ Do not immerse the cord or plug in water.
◇ The breadmaker should be used on a work surface where it cannot be knocked, but not near sources of heat such as the cooker.
◇ Keep the machine out of the reach of children.
◇ Remove the bread pan before adding ingredients, then lock it into position in the machine.
◇ Never insert hands, spoons or any other implement into the machine while it is switched on.
◇ Use oven gloves to remove the pan.
◇ Stand the pan on a heatproof surface.
◇ Do not attempt cleaning until the pan has cooled down.
◇ Clean up any spills inside the machine itself, i.e. by the element, when the machine is switched off, unplugged and has cooled down.
◇ Do not cover the steam vents while in operation.
◇ Do not attempt to move the machine while it is switched on.
◇ Follow the manufacturer's instructions carefully.
◇ Only use the breadmaker for its intended use.

How to use your breadmaker

The first thing to reiterate here is **refer to your instruction manual**; though most breadmakers are similar in their operation, there are variations and if these are not taken into account your results may be disappointing. The following is therefore a guide only. With practice you will develop a safe and effective routine for using your breadmaker.

1. Find a safe place to use your breadmaker.
2. Open the lid and remove the paddle(s) then, using the handle, pull out the bread pan and stand it on a safe, level work surface.
3. Reinsert the paddle(s), checking they are properly engaged.
4. Add the ingredients to the pan in the order listed in the recipe or that recommended in the instruction manual.

NOTE: Some breadmakers recommend adding the dry ingredients first, some the wet: I have tried both methods in a variety of breadmakers and find there is no noticeable difference in the end results. The important factor seems to be keeping the yeast separated from the liquid by the dry ingredients (particularly when delaying the start time). Apart from this, the precise order of adding the ingredients doesn't seem to make a lot of difference.

5. Some manufacturers recommend using tepid water. Although the temperature of the water is essential with the RAPID/FAST cycles, I have found that cold water is just as successful with other cycles.
6. Carefully push the bread pan back down into position in the machine until it clicks in place. Close the lid.
7. Plug in the machine and switch it on at the mains.
8. Set the programme/cycle you require. The instruction booklet will tell you how to do this. You may also have a choice of loaf size and crust colour.
9. Press START.
10. If the recipe includes ingredients that you do not want to become too minced up, e.g. nuts, raisins and olives, then add them when the beeper/buzzer sounds. Apart from this, avoid opening the machine during a cycle as you will release the heat and affect both the proving and cooking temperatures required.
11. At the end of the cycle press STOP and turn off at the mains. Open the lid.
12. Carefully lift out the bread pan using oven gloves and tip the loaf out on to a wire rack to cool.
13. Clean the pan as described earlier.

14. If the paddle has become lodged in the base of the loaf, as I found often happened, hook it out using a wooden or tough plastic implement so that the non-stick surface is not damaged. It is easier to do this while the bread is still warm.
15. Unplug the machine.
16. Slice the bread when cool.

Choosing the right setting

Much of this comes with trial and error, but here are some guidelines for the basic range of programmes.

◇ **Basic:** use this for breads that are made from all or a high proportion of strong plain white flour.

◇ **Wholemeal/wheat:** this cycle is most effective for breads containing wholemeal flour or wholegrain flours such as rye, barley and oats.

◇ **French/continental/speciality:** use this cycle for French breads, Italian breads or breads with very little or no fat.

◇ **Dough:** this programme is used for any recipe where the bread is removed from the pan, shaped and then baked in a conventional oven. The dough generally needs a second rising outside the breadmaker.

◇ **Sweet:** this cycle can be used for breads with a high proportion of sugar such as fruit loaves and some of the enriched doughs.

Some more unusual settings

◇ **Rapid/fast:** very quick cycles that require warm water and fast-acting yeast.

◇ **Cake:** a programme used to bake cakes, which require longer cooking. Good results can be achieved, though the cakes do not have the puffy risen appearance of those cooked by the conventional method.

◇ **Jam:** a useful programme for making small quantities of fruit into jam.

◇ **Pasta:** a useful programme for Italian food enthusiasts.

The successful loaf

Producing a successful loaf is a result of a combination of factors:

◇ Using the breadmaker correctly.
◇ The right choice of ingredients.
◇ Creating the correct conditions and using the correct techniques.

We have already looked at the correct process of using the breadmaker, so I am now going to look at the choice of ingredients. These are not hard and fast rules, but my own findings from experimenting with various breadmakers and ingredients.

Ingredients

Flour

To make successful bread you need to choose flour with a high gluten content. These are known as strong flours, such as strong white or strong wholemeal bread flour. Generally speaking, ordinary plain (all-purpose) flours do not have enough gluten to produce a good, well-risen loaf.

I have found that using all wholemeal or wholegrain flour in a recipe produces a rather stodgy, tough bread. The texture is greatly improved by using half white and half wholemeal or wholegrain flour but, of course, this is again a matter of taste.

◇ Granary flour combined with white bread flour gives a lovely crumbly texture to bread.
◇ Rye flour has a very low gluten content so needs to be supplemented with a bread flour.
◇ Spelt flour, derived from a particular variety of the wheat plant, gives good results in the breadmaker and produces an interesting nutty flavour.
◇ Semolina (cream of wheat) flour also makes an interesting bread and lends itself well to savoury flavourings.

◇ Buckwheat is not strictly a wheat but is the seed of a rhubarb-type plant. As such, it has no gluten and must therefore be used as a flavouring rather than the base flour in a recipe.

◇ Cornmeal adds texture and colour to a standard loaf and is enhanced by spicy flavourings.

◇ Ordinary plain (all-purpose) or self-raising (self-rising) flour should be used in the cake recipes in this book.

Grains

Cereal grains such as oats and barley and also bran etc. may be used in their various forms to both enhance the flavour and texture and add to the nutritional value of the bread. However, too large a proportion of these ingredients may result in heavy bread.

Yeast

Yeast produces carbon dioxide when it is given warmth, time, food and moisture and is essential to make bread. Traditional active dried yeast is used in breadmakers, and I recommend this for all but the RAPID/FAST programmes, for which you must use fast-acting yeast. Fresh yeast is not suitable for use in a breadmaker.

Traditional active dried yeast is the ordinary dried yeast you would normally mix with warm water before adding to the dough, but it is added neat to breadmakers and gives good results. Some manufacturers say fast-acting yeast is suitable for ordinary as well as RAPID/FAST programmes, others that it reacts too quickly and results in a bread that is too 'airy'.

Sourdough

Some recipes, particularly some traditional or foreign ones, require a sourdough starter. If you wish to make use of this, make up a small batch and keep it on hand. Simply mix a cup of flour with a cup of water and stir in a pinch of yeast. Place in a large plastic or glass container and leave unrefrigerated for about a week. The yeast gets to work and produces an small bubbling cauldron! Use some of the sourdough starter at least once a week and replace with equal quantities of flour and water, mixed. After the initial week, the mixture can be stored in the fridge for about two weeks, but ensure it is at room temperature before you use it.

Sweeteners

Most recipes require a small amount of a sweetener of some description to feed the yeast if not to flavour the dough. Some instruction manuals recommend caster (superfine) sugar as it mixes in easily. However, I used granulated sugar successfully in most of my recipes. Brown sugar may also be used. Alternatively, some recipes use honey, which gives a very delicate sweetness, or golden (light corn) syrup. Be fairly accurate in measuring the sweetener or you may end up with a bland or sickly bread.

You may also like to experiment with malt extract, which is a syrup extracted from dried sprouted barley. This adds a sweetness to the bread as well as contributing a malty flavour. It is available from health food shops.

Salt

Salt is included in all the bread recipes as it is essential for adding flavour as well as contributing to the final risen structure of the loaf. As it has a slowing effect on the activity of the yeast, too much salt will kill the yeast, while too little would make the dough rise so fast that it may collapse before it is baked.

Fat

Fat has a shortening property, which gives bread its slightly crumbly texture and also improves its keeping properties. It may be added in the form of oil, margarine, butter or lard (shortening). Oil is easily incorporated in the breadmaker. Sunflower oil contributes little flavour to the bread, while extra virgin olive oil gives a lovely tang to Italian and continental-style bread. It is fine to use margarine suitable for cooking, butter or lard, but ensure that it is softened before being put in the bread pan or it may not mix in properly.

Liquids
The recipes in this book include a range of liquids from water and milk to cider, beer and fruit juice. Most recipes use dried milk powder (non-fat dry milk) and water, which combine in the mixing process to give milk. Ordinary milk can also be used but is not recommended if you wish to use the timer function for a delayed start. It is important that the quantity of liquid used in the recipe is correct, or there can be problems with the shape and texture of the final loaf. Unfortunately, this tends to vary not only from recipe to recipe but also according to the breadmaker you have, the flour used and the cycle selected. Trial and error is really the only answer.

Eggs
Eggs help to give an enriched dough and a more 'cakey' texture. Use fresh eggs and add with the liquid ingredients. It is not advisable to use them with the timer function to delay the start time.

Baking techniques

Having looked at the basic ingredients for bread making, it is important to explain some of the techniques and helpful hints of successful baking with the breadmaker. These are as follows:
◇ Always add ingredients in the order listed OR ensure that the yeast does not come in contact with the liquid as it will start to ferment too quickly.
◇ Ensure that the quantities you use suit the capacity of your breadmaker.
◇ 'Knock back' means giving the dough a few small punches to knock out air pockets.
◇ Don't over-work dough once it comes out of the machine, simply shape it.
◇ Don't over-flour work surfaces as this will dry out the dough and give an unpleasant, heavy texture.
◇ Ensure that baking (cookie) sheets are lightly greased with either a little oil or a smear of margarine or lard (shortening). Do not over-grease as this will give your bread an unpleasant flavour.

◇ 'Proving' dough means putting it in a warm place to allow it to rise. Generally, the dough should nearly double in volume. Never put the dough anywhere hot as this would kill the yeast: similarly, do not put the dough anywhere cold or in a draught as this can kill the yeast or at least slow it down radically.

◇ Always completely cover proving dough. Either use a tea towel (dish cloth), lightly greased clingfilm (plastic wrap) or place the dough inside a greased polythene bag.

◇ Always remove the covering from the dough before it is placed in the oven.

◇ Ensure that your oven is preheated before putting in the dough.

◇ Remove bread from the baking tin (pan) as soon as possible to prevent it going soggy.

◇ Bread slices better once it is cool.

◇ You can vary any of the oven-baked loaves by glazing them to give a shiny finish, or sprinkling them with nuts, seeds or herbs for extra flavour and texture. There are glazing and topping suggestions on page 99.

Timing

Timings vary tremendously between different machines so it is not possible to give useful recipe times. For example, the BASIC programme can take 2½ hours in one machine and 4 hours in another. However, this will give you some idea of how long an average programme should take.

◇ Basic: 2½ hours
◇ Wholemeal/wheat: 2¾ hours
◇ French/continental/speciality: 2¾ hours
◇ Rapid/fast: 1–2 hours
◇ Sweet: 1½ hours
◇ Cake: 2½ hours
◇ Jam: 1 hour
◇ Pasta: 15 minutes

Problems and solutions

Be prepared for a few mishaps! Even if you have followed the recipe meticulously, as mentioned previously breadmakers, their cycles and the ingredients do vary so you may have to make some adjustments. Here are a few common problems and their solutions.

Problem	Causes	Solution
Sunken top	Too wet	Reduce liquid by 15 ml/1 tbsp or increase flour by 30 ml/ 2 tbsp
Mushroom top	Bread has risen too quickly	Reduce yeast by 1.5 ml/¼ tsp or increase salt slightly
Uneven top	Too little moisture	Add 15 ml/1 tbsp water or reduce flour by 30 ml/2 tbsp
Bread has risen too much	Liquid too hot	Use tepid or cold water
	Too much yeast	Measure ingredients accurately
	Too much liquid	Measure ingredients accurately
Bread soggy in middle	Too much syrup from canned fruit	Drain canned fruit thoroughly
	Too high a proportion of rich ingredients (e.g. nuts and grains)	Reduce amount of rich ingredient
Bread has large air holes	Too much liquid or liquid added too hot	Measure accurately and use tepid or cold water
Bread overbrowned	Too much sugar in mixture	Reduce the amount of sugar or sugary ingredients
Bread texture too dense	Not enough liquid	Add an extra 15 ml/1 tbsp water

Your breadmaker storecupboard

*T*he range of ingredients you can use in your breadmaker is limitless, though there are obviously some that form the basis of most bread recipes. The following list gives only a guide to the basic ingredients you may need and also some that I have found useful for flavouring breads. Your choice will depend on your taste and your spirit of adventure.

Dried and packets

◇ Strong white bread flour
◇ Strong wholemeal bread flour
◇ Strong brown bread flour
◇ Malted granary flour
◇ Spelt wheat flour
◇ Rye flour
◇ Barley flour
◇ Buckwheat flour
◇ Cornmeal
◇ Semolina (cream of wheat)
◇ Barley flakes
◇ Cracked wheat
◇ Wheatgerm
◇ Rolled oats
◇ Oatmeal
◇ Traditional active dried yeast
◇ Fast-acting dried yeast
◇ Salt
◇ Sugar: granulated, caster (superfine) and brown
◇ Dried mixed fruit (fruit cake mix)
◇ Raisins
◇ No-need-to-soak dried apricots
◇ No-need-to-soak dried peaches
◇ No-need-to-soak dried pears
◇ Dried figs

◇ Walnut pieces
◇ Almonds: ground, flaked (slivered) and whole blanched
◇ Dried milk powder (non-fat dry milk)
◇ Sesame seeds
◇ Sunflower seeds
◇ Pumpkin seeds

Cans and bottles

◇ Stoned (pitted) olives
◇ Canned anchovies
◇ Bottled tapenade
◇ Canned pineapple

Herbs, flavourings and condiments

◇ Peppercorns
◇ Garlic purée (paste)
◇ Tomato purée
◇ Chutney
◇ Soy sauce
◇ Vinegar
◇ Chilli powder
◇ Curry paste
◇ Dried herbs: oregano, basil, mint, thyme, parsley etc.
◇ Spices: nutmeg, cinnamon, ground ginger, mixed (apple-pie) spice etc.
◇ Honey
◇ Peanut butter
◇ Strawberry jam (conserve)
◇ Golden (light corn) syrup
◇ Mustard powder
◇ Wholegrain mustard
◇ Sunflower oil
◇ Olive oil
◇ Cocoa (unsweetened chocolate) powder
◇ Plain (semi-sweet) chocolate
◇ Pesto

◇ Malt extract
◇ Vanilla essence (extract)
◇ Caraway seeds

Fridge and freezer

◇ Fresh herbs: basil, thyme, parsley, sage, mint, coriander (cilantro) etc.
◇ Eggs
◇ Milk
◇ Butter
◇ Margarine
◇ Lard (shortening)
◇ Garlic
◇ Onions
◇ Potatoes
◇ Strong Cheddar cheese
◇ Blue cheese
◇ Cream cheese
◇ Parmesan cheese
◇ Bacon
◇ Ham
◇ Oranges
◇ Lemons
◇ Limes
◇ Bananas (stored in a cool place)

Storing your bread

*I*deally, eat your bread on the day that you make it. Allow it to cool first on a wire rack, then slice with a very sharp bread knife. However, if this is not possible, you can store bread either in a sealed plastic bag or closely wrapped in clingfilm (plastic wrap), then placed in an airtight container or in the fridge. Home-made bread dries out more quickly than the commercial variety, so it is important to wrap it well.

Bread can also be stored well in the freezer. Allow it to cool thoroughly, then wrap well in clingfilm and place in the freezer. Defrost at room temperature for a couple of hours before eating.

Bread that has dried out can either be used in desserts such as bread and butter pudding and bread pudding or can be made into crumbs and used as a coating for food or in stuffing mixtures.

Notes on the recipes

The following are guidelines to help you with the recipes. The breadmaker manuals and books I have studied all vary in whether they use weighed ingredients or cup measures. I have attempted to give both options for all the recipes, but certain variations occur in translating one to another. It is important therefore to follow one or the other but also to make adjustments to quantities if you find this necessary for your specific breadmaker.

◇ Do not mix metric, imperial and American measures.

◇ All spoon measures are level: 1 tsp = 5 ml; 1 tbsp = 15 ml.

◇ Eggs are medium. If you use a different size, adjust the amount of added liquid accordingly.

◇ Thoroughly prepare fruit and vegetables before you start to assemble your ingredients. NEVER add fruits with stones (pits) to the breadmaker without removing the stones first.

◇ Ensure that flour, yeast and fresh ingredients are in date and in good condition.

◇ Always use fresh herbs where possible, but if you replace them with dried use only half the amount. Dried versions of some herbs, such as parsley and coriander (cilantro), bear little resemblance to fresh and should not be used.

◇ Can and packet sizes are approximate.

◇ Thoroughly drain canned foods first but read the recipe to see if the liquid should be reserved.

◇ Use good-quality oil such as sunflower or olive. Where the recipe specifies olive oil, extra virgin gives the best flavour.

◇ Ensure that margarine is suitable for cooking and that butter and margarine are softened before adding to the breadmaker.

◇ Use your discretion when substituting ingredients in recipes.

◇ Always preheat a conventional oven and cook on the centre shelf. Fan ovens do not require preheating.

◇ Oven temperatures vary so baking times have to be approximate. Adjust cooking times and temperatures according to manufacturer's instructions.

◇ Do not use perishable ingredients such as milk and eggs when using the timer to delay the start time.

◇ Only use fast-acting yeast in the RAPID recipes.

◇ Measure ingredients carefully but make a note on your recipe if you have found it necessary to adjust quantities.

◇ Loaf sizes are designed to give you an approximate guide.

Basic bread recipes

Some basic bread recipes to whet your appetite and give you a feel for how your breadmaker works. These are straightforward recipes that are delicious in their own right, but once you have a feel for the basic techniques, experiment by adding your own flavourings.

Basic white bread
MAKES 1 SMALL, MEDIUM OR LARGE LOAF

I have given separate quantities for small, medium and large loaves so you don't have to do any calculating when making your basic loaves.

Small loaf:
150 ml/¼ pt/⅔ cup water
15 ml/1 tbsp dried milk powder (non-fat dry milk)
15 ml/1 tbsp caster (superfine) sugar
2.5 ml/½ tsp salt
30 ml/2 tbsp sunflower oil
225 g/8 oz/2 cups strong white bread flour
5 ml/1 tsp traditional active dried yeast

Medium loaf:
275 ml/9 fl oz/generous 1 cup water
30 ml/2 tbsp dried milk powder (non-fat dry milk)
20 ml/1½ tbsp caster (superfine) sugar
5 ml/1 tsp salt
40 ml/2½ tbsp sunflower oil
350 g/12 oz/3 cups strong white bread flour
7.5 ml/1½ tsp traditional active dried yeast

Large loaf:
375 ml/13 fl oz/1½ cups water
60 ml/4 tbsp dried milk powder (non-fat dry milk)
45 ml/3 tbsp caster (superfine) sugar
7.5 ml/1½ tsp salt
60 ml/4 tbsp sunflower oil
450 g/1 lb/4 cups strong white bread flour
10 ml/2 tsp traditional active dried yeast

① Place the ingredients in the bread pan in the order listed. Place the pan in the breadmaker, ensuring that it is locked.

② Close the lid, select the BASIC setting and press START.

③ When the cycle is complete, carefully remove the pan using oven gloves. Tip the loaf out on to a cooling rack and allow to cool before slicing.

BASIC SETTING

Brown bread

MAKES 1 SMALL, MEDIUM OR LARGE LOAF

I have given separate quantities for small, medium and large loaves so you don't have to do any calculating when making your basic loaves.

Small loaf:
150 ml/¼ pt/⅔ cup water
15 ml/1 tbsp dried milk powder (non-fat dry milk)
15 ml/1 tbsp caster (superfine) sugar
2.5 ml/½ tsp salt
30 ml/2 tbsp sunflower oil
225 g/8 oz/2 cups strong brown bread flour
5 ml/1 tsp traditional active dried yeast

Medium loaf:
275 ml/9 fl oz/generous 1 cup water
30 ml/2 tbsp dried milk powder (non-fat dry milk)
20 ml/1½ tbsp caster (superfine) sugar
5 ml/1 tsp salt
40 ml/2½ tbsp sunflower oil
350 g/12 oz/3 cups strong brown bread flour
7.5 ml/1½ tsp traditional active dried yeast

Large loaf:
375 ml/13 fl oz/1½ cups water
60 ml/4 tbsp dried milk powder (non-fat dry milk)
45 ml/3 tbsp caster (superfine) sugar
7.5 ml/1½ tsp salt
60 ml/4 tbsp sunflower oil
450 g/1 lb/4 cups strong brown bread flour
10 ml/2 tsp traditional active dried yeast

① Place the ingredients in the bread pan in the order listed. Place the pan in the breadmaker, ensuring that it is locked into position.

② Close the lid, select the BASIC setting and press START.

③ When the cycle is complete, carefully remove the pan using oven gloves.

④ Tip the loaf out on to a cooling rack and allow to cool before slicing.

BASIC SETTING

Variety crown bread
MAKES 1 SMALL LOAF

This is a loaf made up of individual rolls with different toppings.

For the dough:
275 ml/9 fl oz/generous 1 cup water
40 ml/2½ tbsp olive oil
30 ml/2 tbsp dried milk powder (non-fat dry milk)
20 ml/1½ tbsp honey
5 ml/1 tsp salt
100 g/4 oz/1 cup strong white bread flour
100 g/4 oz/1 cup spelt flour
100 g/4 oz/1 cup strong wholemeal bread flour
7.5 ml/1½ tsp traditional active dried yeast
For the toppings:
A little milk
Choose a few from the following: sesame seeds, poppy seeds, sunflower seeds, cracked wheat, pumpkin seeds, grated cheese, crushed peanuts

① To make the dough, place the ingredients in the bread pan in the order listed. Place the pan in the breadmaker, ensuring that it is locked into position.

② Close the lid, select the DOUGH setting and press START.

③ When the cycle is complete, carefully remove the pan and tip the dough out on to a lightly floured work surface.

④ Knock back the dough, then divide into seven equal-sized pieces. Roll each piece into a smooth ball.

⑤ Arrange the rolls on a lightly greased baking (cookie) sheet with one roll in the middle and the others closely packed surrounding it.

⑥ Brush the surface of the rolls with milk, then scatter your selected toppings over the rolls so that people will be able to choose the topping they like.

⑦ Cover loosely with lightly greased clingfilm (plastic wrap) and leave in a warm place to prove for about 20 minutes.

⑧ Bake in a preheated oven at 220°C/425°F/gas mark 7 (fan oven 200°C) for about 20–25 minutes.

DOUGH SETTING
PLUS 50 MINUTES SHAPING, RISING AND BAKING

Light wholemeal bread
MAKES 1 SMALL, MEDIUM OR LARGE LOAF

*You could try making this bread using all wholemeal flour,
but this results in heavier bread than the recipe given here.
I have given separate quantities for small, medium and large
loaves so you don't have to do any calculating when making
your basic loaves.*

Small loaf:
150 ml/¼ pt/⅔ cup water
15 ml/1 tbsp dried milk powder (non-fat dry milk)
15 ml/1 tbsp caster (superfine) sugar
2.5 ml/½ tsp salt
30 ml/2 tbsp sunflower oil
100 g/4 oz/1 cup strong white bread flour
100 g/4 oz/1 cup strong wholemeal bread flour
5 ml/1 tsp traditional active dried yeast

Medium loaf:
275 ml/9 fl oz/generous 1 cup water
30 ml/2 tbsp dried milk powder (non-fat dry milk)
20 ml/1½ tbsp caster (superfine) sugar
5 ml/1 tsp salt
40 ml/2½ tbsp sunflower oil
175 g/6 oz/1½ cups strong white bread flour
175 g/6 oz/1½ cups strong wholemeal bread flour
7.5 ml/1½ tsp traditional active dried yeast

Large loaf:
375 ml/13 fl oz/1½ cups water
60 ml/4 tbsp dried milk powder (non-fat dry milk)
45 ml/3 tbsp caster (superfine) sugar
7.5 ml/1½ tsp salt
60 ml/4 tbsp sunflower oil
225 g/8 oz/2 cups strong white bread flour
225 g/8 oz/2 cups strong wholemeal bread flour
10 ml/2 tsp traditional active dried yeast

① Place the ingredients in the bread pan in the order listed. Place the pan in the breadmaker, ensuring that it is locked into position.

② Close the lid, select the WHOLEMEAL setting and press START.

③ When the cycle is complete, carefully remove the pan using oven gloves.

④ Tip the loaf out on to a cooling rack and allow to cool before slicing.

WHOLEMEAL SETTING

Grain breads

A selection of bread recipes using an assortment of different grains. Dabble with wheat, oats, barley and a range of flours to discover the different flavours and textures they produce. Visit any good wholefood or health food store to discover other unusual grains and flours you may like to try.

Cheese and mint semolina bread
MAKES 1 LARGE LOAF

This is an unusual bread based on a Middle Eastern recipe. It makes a good side dish to the spicy soups and stews from this part of the world.

300 ml/½ pt/1¼ cups water
45 ml/3 tbsp sunflower oil
A good handful of fresh mint leaves
7.5 ml/1½ tsp salt
7.5 ml/1½ tsp sugar
100 g/4 oz/1 cup strong Cheddar cheese, grated
400 g/14 oz/3½ cups semolina (cream of wheat) flour
10 ml/2 tsp traditional active dried yeast

① Place the ingredients in the bread pan in the order listed. Place the pan in the breadmaker, ensuring that it is locked into position.

② Close the lid, select the BASIC setting and press START.

③ When the cycle is complete, carefully remove the pan using oven gloves.

④ Tip the loaf out on to a cooling rack and allow to cool before slicing.

BASIC SETTING

Malted oat loaf

MAKES 1 MEDIUM LOAF

A healthy, crumbly bread. Enjoy with fresh fruit and cheese.

350 ml/12 fl oz/1⅓ cups water
30 ml/2 tbsp sunflower oil
30 ml/2 tbsp malt extract
60 ml/4 tbsp dried milk powder (non-fat dry milk)
7.5 ml/1½ tsp salt
300 g/11 oz/2¾ cups strong white bread flour
175 g/6 oz/1½ cups rolled oats
10 ml/2 tsp traditional active dried yeast

① Place the ingredients in the bread pan in the order listed. Place the pan in the breadmaker, ensuring that it is locked into position.

② Close the lid, select the BASIC setting and press START.

③ When the cycle is complete, carefully remove the pan using oven gloves.

④ Tip the loaf out on to a cooling rack and allow to cool before slicing.

BASIC SETTING

Malted bran loaf
MAKES 1 MEDIUM LOAF

This tasty bread is lovely sliced and buttered at teatime but is also delicious toasted and buttered for breakfast. Rolled bran flakes are available from health food stores.

350 ml/12 fl oz/1⅓ cups water
30 ml/2 tbsp sunflower oil
30 ml/2 tbsp malt extract
60 ml/4 tbsp dried milk powder (non-fat dry milk)
7.5 ml/1½ tsp salt
300 g/11 oz/2¾ cups strong white bread flour
175 g/6 oz/1½ cups rolled bran flakes
5 ml/1 tsp traditional active dried yeast

① Place the ingredients in the bread pan in the order listed. Place the pan in the breadmaker, ensuring that it is locked into position.

② Close the lid, select the BASIC setting and press START.

③ When the cycle is complete, carefully remove the pan using oven gloves.

④ Tip the loaf out on to a cooling rack and allow to cool before slicing.

BASIC SETTING

Rye bread
MAKES 1 MEDIUM LOAF

This is quite a heavy bread, which is excellent for using as a base for open sandwiches.

250 ml/8 fl oz/1 cup water
15 ml/1 tbsp margarine
5 ml/1 tsp caster (superfine) sugar
10 ml/2 tsp salt
225 g/8 oz/2 cups strong white bread flour
225 g/8 oz/2 cups rye flour
7.5 ml/1½ tsp traditional active dried yeast

① Place the ingredients in the bread pan in the order listed. Place the pan in the breadmaker, ensuring that it is locked into position.

② Close the lid, select the WHOLEMEAL setting and press START.

③ When the cycle is complete, carefully remove the pan using oven gloves.

④ Tip the loaf out on to a cooling rack and allow to cool before slicing.

WHOLEMEAL SETTING

Rye, onion, potato and fennel loaf
MAKES 1 MEDIUM LOAF

A moist, close-textured bread that lends itself equally well as an accompaniment to cheese and pickles as soups and stews.

250 ml/8 fl oz/1 cup water
30 ml/2 tbsp sunflower oil
60 ml/4 tbsp vinegar
7.5 ml/1½ tsp salt
30 ml/2 tbsp sugar
30 ml/2 tbsp fennel seeds
1 large onion, grated
1 raw unpeeled boiling potato, grated
350 g/12 oz/3 cups strong white bread flour
100 g/4 oz/1 cup rye flour
10 ml/2 tsp traditional active dried yeast

① Place the ingredients in the bread pan in the order listed. Place the pan in the breadmaker, ensuring that it is locked into position.

② Close the lid, select the WHOLEMEAL setting and press START.

③ When the cycle is complete, carefully remove the pan using oven gloves.

④ Tip the loaf out on to a cooling rack and allow to cool before slicing.

WHOLEMEAL SETTING

Carrot and fancy mustard bread

MAKES 1 SMALL LOAF

Try this with soup or grilled (broiled) meat or fish.

---

275 ml/9 fl oz/generous 1 cup water
275 g/10 oz/1⅔ cups carrots, grated
60 ml/4 tbsp tomato and basil mustard with honey or
** your favourite mustard**
20 ml/1½ tbsp sunflower oil
20 ml/1½ tbsp caster (superfine) sugar
5 ml/1 tsp salt
225 g/8 oz/2 cups strong white bread flour
100 g/4 oz/1 cup strong wholemeal bread flour
50 g/2 oz/½ cup yellow cornmeal
7.5 ml/1½ tsp traditional active dried yeast

---

① Place the ingredients in the bread pan in the order listed. Place the pan in the breadmaker, ensuring that it is locked into position.

② Close the lid, select the WHOLEMEAL setting and press START.

③ When the cycle is complete, carefully remove the pan using oven gloves.

④ Tip the loaf out on to a cooling rack and allow to cool before slicing.

WHOLEMEAL SETTING

Buckwheat and Italian bean roll
MAKES 1 MEDIUM LOAF

This bread has a strong flavour, good with cheeses and ham.

For the dough:
275 ml/9 fl oz/generous 1 cup water
20 ml/1½ tbsp sunflower oil
30 ml/2 tbsp dried milk powder (non-fat dry milk)
20 ml/1½ tbsp caster (superfine) sugar
5 ml/1 tsp salt
350 g/12 oz/3 cups strong white bread flour
100 g/4 oz/1 cup buckwheat flour
10 ml/2 tsp traditional active dried yeast
For the filling:
300 g/11 oz/1 medium can of Italian beans in sauce

① To make the dough, place the ingredients in the bread pan in the order listed. Place the pan in the breadmaker, ensuring that it is locked into position.

② Close the lid, select the DOUGH setting and press START.

③ When the cycle is complete, carefully remove the pan and tip the dough out on to a lightly floured work surface.

④ Knock back the dough, then roll out to a little larger than a sheet of A4 paper. Spread the beans over the surface and roll up along the long edge.

⑤ Place on a lightly greased baking (cookie) sheet with the join underneath. Cover with lightly greased clingfilm (plastic wrap) and leave in a warm place to prove for about 30 minutes.

⑥ Bake in a preheated oven at 200°C/400°F/gas mark 6 (fan oven 180°C) for about 20 minutes.

⑦ Tip the loaf out on to a cooling rack and allow to cool before slicing.

DOUGH SETTING
PLUS 1 HOUR, SHAPING, RISING AND BAKING

Spelt bread with sesame seeds
MAKES 2 SMALL LOAVES

This bread has a thick crispy crust and a pronounced wheaty flavour. The dough is quite runny and needs to be poured.

400 ml/14 fl oz/1¾ cups water
15 ml/1 tbsp honey
7.5 ml/1½ tsp salt
15 ml/1 tbsp margarine
225 g/8 oz/2 cups strong white bread flour
225 g/8 oz/2 cups spelt flour
7.5 ml/1½ tsp traditional active dried yeast
30 ml/2 tbsp sesame seeds

① Place all the ingredients except the sesame seeds in the bread pan in the order listed. Place the pan in the breadmaker, ensuring that it is locked into position.

② Close the lid, select the DOUGH programme and press START.

③ When the cycle is complete, carefully remove the pan and pour the dough into two lightly greased 450 g/1 lb loaf tins (pans).

④ Sprinkle with the sesame seeds, cover loosely with lightly greased clingfilm (plastic wrap) and leave in a warm place to prove for 15 minutes.

⑤ Bake in a preheated oven at 190°C/375°F/gas mark 5 (fan oven 170°C) for about 45 minutes.

⑥ Tip the loaf out on to a cooling rack and allow to cool before slicing.

DOUGH SETTING
PLUS 1HOUR SHAPING, RISING AND BAKING

Sun-dried tomato and rosemary oat bread

MAKES 1 MEDIUM LOAF

A really 'gutsy' bread and a good accompaniment to grilled (broiled) meat or fish.

100 g/4 oz sun-dried tomatoes
250 ml/8 fl oz/1 cup warm water
30 ml/2 tbsp olive oil
A good handful of fresh rosemary sprigs
7.5 ml/1½ tsp salt
15 ml/1 tbsp sugar
375 g/13 oz/3¼ cups strong white bread flour
125 g/4½ oz/1 cup + 2 tbsp rolled oats
5 ml/1 tsp traditional active dried yeast

① Soak the tomatoes in the warm water for 15 minutes. Allow to cool.

② Place the tomatoes and the soaking water in the bread pan and add all the remaining ingredients in the order listed. Place the pan in the breadmaker, ensuring that it is locked into position.

③ Close the lid, select the WHOLEMEAL setting and press START.

④ When the cycle is complete, carefully remove the pan using oven gloves.

⑤ Tip the loaf out on to a cooling rack and allow to cool before slicing.

WHOLEMEAL SETTING

Very light seed and granary loaf

MAKES 1 MEDIUM LOAF

This recipe gives a smallish amount of dough, but don't try increasing the quantities because the loaf rises so well it fills a standard breadmaker!

275 ml/9 fl oz/generous 1 cup water
15 ml/1 tbsp dried milk powder (non-fat dry milk)
40 ml/2½ tbsp soft brown sugar
5 ml/1 tsp salt
30 ml/2 tbsp sunflower oil
225 g/8 oz/2 cups strong white bread flour
100 g/4 oz/1 cup granary flour
15 ml/1 tbsp sesame seeds
15 ml/1 tbsp pumpkin seeds
15 ml/1 tbsp sunflower seeds
6 ml/1¼ tsp traditional active dried yeast

① Place the ingredients in the bread pan in the order listed. Place the pan in the breadmaker, ensuring that it is locked into position.

② Close the lid, select the WHOLEMEAL setting and press START.

③ When the cycle is complete, carefully remove the pan using oven gloves.

④ Tip the loaf out on to a cooling rack and allow to cool before slicing.

WHOLEMEAL SETTING

Granary bread
MAKES 1 MEDIUM LOAF

---

275 ml/9 fl oz/generous 1 cup water
30 ml/2 tbsp dried milk powder (non-fat dry milk)
20 ml/1½ tbsp caster (superfine) sugar
5 ml/1 tsp salt
40 ml/2½ tbsp sunflower oil
175 g/6 oz/1½ cups strong white bread flour
175 g/6 oz/1½ cups granary flour
6 ml/1¼ tsp traditional active dried yeast

---

① Place the ingredients in the bread pan in the order listed. Place the pan in the breadmaker, ensuring that it is locked into position.

② Close the lid, select the WHOLEMEAL setting and press START.

③ When the cycle is complete, carefully remove the pan using oven gloves.

④ Tip the loaf out on to a cooling rack and allow to cool before slicing.

WHOLEMEAL SETTING

Oatmeal sourdough bread
MAKES 1 SMALL LOAF

I find this small loaf adequate for my family as this is such a filling bread. However, if you require a larger loaf increase the quantities proportionally.

---

120 ml/4 fl oz/½ cup milk
100 g/4 oz/1 cup oatmeal
60 ml/4 tbsp sourdough starter (page 15)
60 ml/4 tbsp water
5 ml/1 tsp honey
2.5 ml/½ tsp salt
175 g/6 oz/1½ cups strong white bread flour
5 ml/1 tsp traditional active dried yeast

---

① Place the ingredients in the bread pan in the order listed. Place the pan in the breadmaker, ensuring that it is locked into position.

② Close the lid, select the WHOLEMEAL setting and press START.

③ When the cycle is complete, carefully remove the pan using oven gloves.

④ Tip the loaf out on to a cooling rack and allow to cool before slicing.

WHOLEMEAL SETTING

Mango, banana and seed loaf
MAKES 1 LARGE LOAF

This is moist tea bread, which is as good eaten for breakfast as for afternoon tea! Serve as it is or with butter and runny honey.

---

100 g/4 oz/1 cup sun-dried mango
300 ml/½ pt/1¼ cups cold water
15 ml/1 tbsp sunflower oil
1 banana, mashed
5 ml/1 tsp salt
30 ml/2 tbsp sugar
30 ml/2 tbsp dried milk powder (non-fat dry milk)
450 g/1 lb/4 cups strong white bread flour
5 ml/1 tsp ground cinnamon
5 ml/1 tsp traditional active dried yeast
25 g/1 oz/¼ cup pumpkin seeds
25 g/1 oz/¼ cup sunflower seeds

---

① Soak the mango in enough warm water to cover for about 15 minutes.

② Place all the remaining ingredients except the seeds in the bread pan in the order listed. Place the pan in the breadmaker, ensuring that it is locked into position.

③ Close the lid, select the BASIC setting and press START.

④ Drain the water from the mango. Add the mango and seeds at the buzzer or after the first kneading.

⑤ When the cycle is complete, carefully remove the pan using oven gloves.

⑥ Tip the loaf out on to a cooling rack and allow to cool before slicing.

BASIC SETTING

Savoury breads

*T*his chapter offers a whole host of ideas for savoury breads – the problem is knowing when to stop experimenting with flavours! Strong flavours work well in bread and it is important to remember that the flour tends to absorb and dilute flavours, so be bold and use strong cheeses, punchy herbs and spices and lingering flavours.

Savoury cheese wheels
MAKES ABOUT 20

For the dough:
275 ml/9 fl oz/generous 1 cup water
40 ml/2½ tbsp olive oil
30 ml/2 tbsp dried milk powder (non-fat dry milk)
20 ml/1½ tbsp honey
5 ml/1 tsp salt
100 g/4 oz/1 cup strong white bread flour
100 g/4 oz/1 cup spelt flour
100 g/4 oz/1 cup strong wholemeal bread flour
7.5 ml/1½ tsp traditional active dried yeast
For the filling:
30 ml/2 tbsp yeast extract
175 g/6 oz/1½ cups strong cheese, grated

① To make the dough, place the ingredients in the bread pan in the order listed. Place the pan in the breadmaker, ensuring that it is locked into position.

② Close the lid, select the DOUGH setting and press START.

③ When the cycle is complete, carefully remove the pan and tip the dough out on to a lightly floured work surface.

④ Knock back the dough, then roll out to a square about 35 x 35 cm/14 x 14 in. Spread the dough with the yeast extract, then sprinkle the cheese over.

⑤ Roll up tightly, then cut the roll into about 20 thin slices with a sharp knife. Place the slices flat-side down on a lightly greased baking (cookie) sheet.

⑥ Cover loosely with lightly greased clingfilm (plastic wrap) and leave in a warm place to prove for about 10 minutes.

⑦ Bake in a preheated oven at 200°C/400°F/gas mark 6 (fan oven 180°C) for about 5–10 minutes.

DOUGH SETTING
PLUS 30 MINUTES SHAPING, RISING AND BAKING

Petits pains with pineapple cheese filling
MAKES 12

These little rolls are great for picnics or eaten as a snack, warm from the oven. The delicious rings of pineapple-flavoured cream cheese covered in chopped nuts that I use in this recipe are readily available in major supermarkets.

250 ml/8 fl oz/1 cup water
45 ml/3 tbsp oil
7.5 ml/1½ tsp salt
15 ml/1 tbsp sugar
450 g/1 lb/4 cups strong white bread flour
5 ml/1 tsp traditional active dried yeast
2 pineapple cheese rings, each cut into six pieces

① Place all the ingredients except the cheese in the bread pan in the order listed. Place the pan in the breadmaker, ensuring that it is locked into position.

② Close the lid, select the DOUGH setting and press START.

③ When the cycle is complete, carefully remove the pan and tip the dough out on to a lightly floured work surface.

④ Knock back the dough, then divide it into 12 equal-sized pieces. Form into balls, then flatten them slightly.

⑤ Place one of the pieces of cheese in the middle of each ball and pull the dough up around the cheese. Pinch well to seal.

⑥ Turn over and place, sealed-side down, on a lightly greased baking (cookie) sheet.

⑦ Cover loosely with clingfilm (plastic wrap) and leave in a warm place to prove for about 20 minutes.

⑧ Bake the rolls in a preheated oven at 190°C/325°F/gas mark 5 (fan oven 170°C) for about 10 minutes until golden brown.

DOUGH SETTING
PLUS 40 MINUTES SHAPING, RISING AND BAKING

Tapenade bread
MAKES 1 LARGE LOAF

I used olive, lemon and garlic tapenade for this bread, but you can use your own favourite.

275 ml/9 fl oz/generous 1 cup water
20 ml/1½ tbsp olive oil
5 ml/1 tsp sugar
5 ml/1 tsp salt
2.5 ml/½ tsp freshly ground black pepper
90 ml/6 tbsp tapenade
225 g/8 oz/2 cups strong white bread flour
100 g/4 oz/1 cup strong wholemeal bread flour
75 g/3 oz/¾ cup malted granary flour
10 ml/2 tsp traditional active dried yeast

① Place all the ingredients in the bread pan in the order listed. Place the pan in the breadmaker, ensuring that it is locked into position.

② Close the lid, select the WHOLEMEAL setting and press START.

③ When the cycle is complete, carefully remove the pan using oven gloves.

④ Tip the loaf out on to a cooling rack and allow to cool before slicing.

WHOLEMEAL SETTING

Courgette and tomato bread
MAKES 1 LARGE LOAF

This is a moist bread, best eaten warm from the oven with either grilled (broiled) meat or a large chunk of Brie.

For the flavouring:
15 ml/1 tbsp oil
1 shallot, chopped
1 courgette (zucchini), diced
2 large tomatoes, sliced
30 ml/2 tbsp tomato purée (paste)
10 basil leaves, torn
Salt and freshly ground black pepper
For the dough:
100 ml/3½ fl oz/scant ½ cup water
30 ml/2 tbsp olive oil
10 ml/2 tsp sugar
7.5 ml/1½ tsp salt
2.5 ml/½ tsp freshly ground black pepper
400 g/14 oz/3½ cups strong white bread flour
10 ml/2 tsp traditional active dried yeast

① To make the flavouring, heat the oil in a frying pan (skillet). Add the shallot and courgette and cook gently until softened.

② Stir in the tomato slices and continue to cook until pulpy.

③ Stir in the tomato purée and basil and season to taste.

④ Place the mixture in the bread pan, then add all the dough ingredients in the order listed. Place the pan in the breadmaker, ensuring that it is locked into position.

⑤ Close the lid, select the FRENCH or BASIC setting and press START.

⑥ When the cycle is complete, carefully remove the pan using oven gloves.

⑦ Tip the loaf out on to a cooling rack and allow to cool before slicing.

FRENCH OR BASIC SETTING

Chilli avocado bread

MAKES 1 LARGE LOAF

A Mexican-style bread that is ideal for serving with dips or spare ribs.

175 ml/6 fl oz/¾ cup water
20 ml/1½ tbsp olive oil
1 small ripe avocado pear, skinned and stoned (pitted)
75 g/3 oz cold fried (sautéed) tomatoes
10 ml/2 tsp sugar
5 ml/1 tsp salt
2.5 ml/½ tsp freshly ground black pepper
10 ml/2 tsp chilli powder
350 g/12 oz/3 cups strong white bread flour
75 g/3 oz/¾ cup malted granary flour
10 ml/2 tsp traditional active dried yeast

① Place all the ingredients in the bread pan in the order listed. Place the pan in the breadmaker, ensuring that it is locked into position.

② Close the lid, select the FRENCH or BASIC setting and press START.

③ When the cycle is complete, carefully remove the pan using oven gloves.

④ Tip the loaf out on to a cooling rack and allow to cool before slicing.

FRENCH OR BASIC SETTING
PLUS 15 MINUTES PRECOOKING

Hawaiian bread
MAKES 1 MEDIUM LOAF

Choose a really strong cheese for this recipe, such as a farmhouse Cheddar, for maximum flavour.

225 g/8 oz/1 small can of pineapple pieces, drained and juice reserved
30 ml/2 tbsp sunflower oil
175 g/6 oz/1½ cups strong cheese, grated
5 ml/1 tsp salt
350 g/12 oz/3 cups strong white bread flour
7.5 ml/1½ tsp traditional active dried yeast
About 6 small slices of ham, chopped

① Make up the reserved pineapple juice to 175 ml/6 fl oz/¾ cup with water. Pour into the bread pan, then add all the remaining ingredients except the ham in the order listed.

② Place the pan in the breadmaker, ensuring that it is locked into position.

③ Close the lid, select the BASIC setting and press START.

④ Add the ham at the buzzer or after the first kneading.

⑤ When the cycle is complete, carefully remove the pan using oven gloves.

⑥ Tip the loaf out on to a cooling rack and allow to cool before slicing.

BASIC SETTING

Blue cheese and walnut bread

MAKES 1 LARGE LOAF

Delicious with cold meats or with cheese and fresh fruit.

350 ml/12 fl oz/1⅓ cups water
25 g/1 oz/2 tbsp butter
175 g/6 oz/1½ cups strong blue cheese, crumbled
15 ml/1 tbsp caster (superfine) sugar
15 ml/1 tbsp dried milk powder (non-fat dry milk)
7.5 ml/1½ tsp salt
225 g/8 oz/2 cups strong white bread flour
225 g/8 oz/2 cups strong wholemeal bread flour
7.5 ml/1½ tsp traditional active dried yeast
100 g/4 oz/1 cup walnuts

① Place all the ingredients except the nuts in the bread pan in the order listed. Place the pan in the breadmaker, ensuring that it is locked into position.

② Close the lid, select the WHOLEMEAL setting and press START.

③ Add the nuts at the buzzer or after the first kneading.

④ When the cycle is complete, carefully remove the pan using oven gloves.

⑤ Tip the loaf out on to a cooling rack and allow to cool before slicing.

WHOLEMEAL SETTING

Cheese and bean bread
MAKES 1 LARGE LOAF

Choose a really strong-flavoured cheese for this recipe, such as a farmhouse Cheddar, for maximum flavour.

275 ml/9 fl oz/generous 1 cup water
45 ml/3 tbsp sunflower oil
175 g/6 oz/1½ cups strong cheese, grated
30 ml/2 tbsp wholegrain mustard
45 ml/3 tbsp dried milk powder (non-fat dry milk)
7.5 ml/1½ tsp salt
20 ml/1½ tbsp sugar
350 g/12 oz/3 cups strong white bread flour
75 g/3 oz/¾ cup granary flour
7.5 ml/1½ tsp traditional active dried yeast
175 g/6 oz cold cooked French (green) beans, chopped

1. Place all the ingredients except the beans in the bread pan in the order listed. Place the pan in the breadmaker, ensuring that it is locked into position.

2. Close the lid, select the BASIC setting and press START.

3. Add the beans at the buzzer or after the first kneading.

4. When the cycle is complete, carefully remove the pan using oven gloves.

5. Tip the loaf out on to a cooling rack and allow to cool before slicing.

BASIC SETTING

fast basil, chive and cheese bread
MAKES 1 MEDIUM LOAF

This bread is made using the RAPID cycle, which many breadmakers have. It is important to use fast-acting yeast and warm (30–35°C/85–95°F) water for the bread to be successful.

275 ml/9 fl oz/generous 1 cup warm water
45 ml/3 tbsp sunflower oil
175 g/6 oz/1½ cups strong cheese, grated
A good handful of fresh basil leaves
60 ml/4 tbsp snipped fresh chives
30 ml/2 tbsp dried milk powder (non-fat dry milk)
5 ml/1 tsp salt
10 ml/2 tsp sugar
350 g/12 oz/3 cups strong white bread flour
7.5 ml/1½ tsp fast-acting yeast

① Place all the ingredients in the bread pan in the order listed. Place the pan in the breadmaker, ensuring that it is locked into position.

② Close the lid, select the RAPID setting and press START.

③ When the cycle is complete, carefully remove the pan using oven gloves.

④ Tip the loaf out on to a cooling rack and allow to cool before slicing.

RAPID SETTING

Sausage and apple roll
MAKES 2

This is great cold for a picnic or a summer buffet.
Alternatively, eat it warm with seasonal vegetables.

For the dough:
300 ml/½ pt/1¼ cups water
30 ml/2 tbsp margarine
10 ml/2 tsp mixed dried herbs
7.5 ml/1½ tsp salt
10 ml/2 tsp sugar
15 ml/1 tbsp dried milk powder (non-fat dry milk)
450 g/1 lb/4 cups strong white bread flour
5 ml/1 tsp traditional active dried yeast
For the filling:
750 g/1¾ lb sausagemeat
2 onions, finely chopped
2 eating (dessert) apples, peeled, cored and finely
  chopped
Salt and freshly ground black pepper
For the glaze:
1 egg, beaten
10 ml/2 tsp water

① To make the dough, place all the ingredients in the bread pan in the order listed. Place the pan in the breadmaker, ensuring that it is locked into position.

② Close the lid, select the DOUGH setting and press START.

③ When the cycle is complete, carefully remove the pan and tip the dough out on to a lightly floured work surface.

④ Knock back the dough, then cut it into two equal-sized pieces.

⑤ Cover loosely with clingfilm (plastic wrap) and leave in a warm place to prove for about 15 minutes.

⑥ Roll out each piece of dough to just larger than a sheet of A4 paper.

⑦ To make the filling, divide the sausagemeat into two pieces, form into long sausages and arrange lengthways in the centre of each piece of dough. Sprinkle the onion and apple equally over each sausage and season with salt and pepper.

⑧ To make the glaze, mix together the egg and water and brush round the edges of the dough. Pull up the edges and pinch well to seal completely, giving two long rolls. Brush all over the surface with the egg glaze.

⑨ Place on oiled baking (cookie) sheets and cook in a preheated oven at 190°C/375°F/gas mark 5 (fan oven 170°C) for about 30 minutes until golden brown.

⑩ Serve thickly sliced.

DOUGH SETTING
PLUS 55 MINUTES SHAPING, RISING AND BAKING

Savoury monkey bread
MAKES 1 MEDIUM LOAF

This 'pull-apart' bread is ideal for picnics or as an accompaniment to meat, fish and pasta dishes.

For the dough:
250 ml/8 fl oz/1 cup water
2 eggs
45 ml/3 tbsp butter
1 red onion, chopped
15 ml/1 tbsp caster (superfine) sugar
5 ml/1 tsp salt
275 g/10 oz/2½ cups strong white bread flour
50 g/2 oz/½ cup granary flour
10 ml/2 tsp traditional active dried yeast
For the glaze:
90 ml/6 tbsp butter
1 garlic clove, crushed
15 ml/1 tbsp chopped fresh parsley

① To make the dough, place all the ingredients in the bread pan in the order listed. Place the pan in the breadmaker, ensuring that it is locked into position.

② Close the lid, select the DOUGH setting and press START.

③ When the cycle is complete, carefully remove the pan and tip the dough out on to a lightly floured work surface.

④ Knock back the dough, then divide into 12 equal-sized pieces. Roll each one into a small ball.

⑤ Melt the butter for the glaze and use a little to grease a 25 cm/10 in tube pan or ring cake tin (pan).

⑥ Combine the remaining butter with the other glaze ingredients. Dip each dough ball in the glaze, then place half of them about 2½ cm/2 in apart in the prepared tin.

⑦ Use the remaining balls to form a second layer, placing them in the gaps.

⑧ Cover loosely with lightly greased clingfilm (plastic wrap) and leave in a warm place to prove for about 20 minutes or until doubled in size.

⑨ Bake in a preheated oven at 180°C/350°F/gas mark 4 (fan oven 160°C) for about 25–30 minutes.

⑩ Remove from the pan and eat either warm or cold.

DOUGH SETTING
PLUS 1 HOUR SHAPING, RISING AND BAKING

Onion and black pepper bread
MAKES 1 LARGE LOAF

This bread is wonderful just eaten warm on its own but also makes a good accompaniment to soups and salads.

For the dough:
300 ml/½ pt/1¼ cups water
30 ml/2 tbsp sunflower oil
7.5 ml/1½ tsp salt
10 ml/2 tsp sugar
15 ml/1 tbsp dried milk powder (non-fat dry milk)
450 g/1 lb/4 cups strong white bread flour
7.5 ml/1½ tsp traditional active dried yeast
For the filling:
6 onions, finely chopped
15 ml/1 tbsp olive oil
10 ml/2 tsp crushed black peppercorns
Milk, for brushing

① To make the dough, place all the ingredients in the bread pan in the order listed. Place the pan in the breadmaker, ensuring that it is locked into position.

② Close the lid, select the DOUGH setting and press START.

③ Meanwhile, to make the filling, sweat the onions in the oil in a lidded pan until very soft. Stir in the crushed peppercorns and allow to cool.

④ When the cycle is complete, carefully remove the pan and tip the dough out on to a lightly floured work surface.

⑤ Knock back the dough, then roll it out into a rectangle a little bigger than a sheet of A4 paper.

⑥ Spoon the onion mixture down the length of the dough in the middle. Using a sharp knife, make long diagonal cuts down the side of the onion mixture as shown.

⑦ Brush the dough with a little water then, starting from the top, alternately fold over the strips, tucking in excess dough at the top and bottom.

⑧ Brush all over with milk and place on a lightly greased baking (cookie) sheet. Cover loosely with clingfilm (plastic wrap) and leave in a warm place to prove for about 30 minutes.

⑨ Bake in a preheated oven at 200°C/400°F/gas mark 6 (fan oven 180°C) for about 20 minutes until golden and puffy.

⑩ Slice thickly and serve while still warm.

DOUGH SETTING
PLUS 1 HOUR SHAPING, RISING AND BAKING

Mango chutney and cheese fries

MAKES 12

These make an excellent summer lunch with a crisp salad.

For the dough:
275 ml/9 fl oz/generous 1 cup water
30 ml/2 tbsp dried milk powder (non-fat dry milk)
20 ml/1½ tbsp caster (superfine) sugar
5 ml/1 tsp salt
40 ml/2½ tbsp sunflower oil
350 g/12 oz/3 cups strong white bread flour
6 ml/1¼ tsp traditional active dried yeast
For the filling:
60 ml/4 tbsp mango chutney
150 g/5 oz/1¼ cups Cheddar cheese, grated
Oil, for deep-frying
60 ml/4 tbsp Parmesan cheese, finely grated

① To make the dough, place all the ingredients in the bread pan in the order listed. Place the pan in the breadmaker, ensuring that it is locked into position.

② Close the lid, select the DOUGH setting and press START.

③ When the cycle is complete, carefully remove the pan and turn the dough out on to a lightly floured work surface.

④ Knock back the dough, then form into 12 equal-sized balls. Press each ball out flat.

⑤ To make the filling, place 5 ml/1 tsp of chutney in the centre of each. Divide the Cheddar cheese between the rounds, being careful not to over-fill. Dampen the edges with water, then pinch the edges up around the filling to seal.

⑥ Cover with lightly greased clingfilm (plastic wrap) and leave in a warm place to prove for about 20 minutes.

⑦ Heat the oil in a large saucepan or deep-fat fryer to just below smoking point.

⑧ Carefully fry (sauté) a few at a time for a few minutes until golden brown, then drain on kitchen paper (paper towels).

⑨ Roll the fries in the Parmesan while still hot.

DOUGH SETTING
PLUS 40 MINUTES SHAPING, RISING AND COOKING

Ploughman's bread
MAKES 1 LARGE LOAF

This bread makes an ideal lunch with plenty of strong Cheddar cheese.

---

375 ml/13 fl oz/1½ cups water
15 ml/1 tbsp sunflower oil
5 ml/1 tsp salt
15 ml/1 tbsp sugar
15 ml/1 tbsp dried milk powder (non-fat dry milk)
100 g/4 oz pickled onions, halved
175 g/6 oz/1½ cups strong Cheddar cheese, grated
225 g/8 oz/2 cups strong white bread flour
225 g/8 oz/2 cups granary flour
7.5 ml/1½ tsp traditional active dried yeast

---

① Place the ingredients in the bread pan in the order listed. Place the pan in the breadmaker, ensuring that it is locked into position.

② Close the lid, select the BASIC setting and press START.

③ When the cycle is complete, carefully remove the pan using oven gloves.

④ Tip the loaf out on to a cooling rack and allow to cool before slicing.

BASIC SETTING

Lemon, Parmesan and black pepper bread

MAKES 1 MEDIUM LOAF

This is a lovely bread to eat warm with pasta dishes and Mediterranean vegetables.

For the dough:
275 ml/9 fl oz/generous 1 cup water
30 ml/2 tbsp dried milk powder (non-fat dry milk)
20 ml/1½ tbsp caster sugar
5 ml/1 tsp salt
40 ml/2½ tbsp extra virgin olive oil
350 g/12 oz/3 cups strong white bread flour
6 ml/1¼ tsp traditional active dried yeast
For the topping:
Zest and juice of 1 lemon
30 ml/2 tbsp extra virgin olive oil
15 ml/1 tbsp black peppercorns, crushed
15 ml/1 tbsp chopped fresh thyme
30 ml/2 tbsp Parmesan cheese, finely grated

① To make the dough, place all the ingredients in the bread pan in the order listed. Place the pan in the breadmaker, ensuring that it is locked into position.

② Close the lid, select the DOUGH setting and press START.

③ When the cycle is complete, carefully remove the pan and tip the dough out on to a lightly floured work surface.

④ Knock back the dough, then form into a large ball. Using sharp scissors, snip into the dough to form 'spikes'.

⑤ To make the topping, combine all the ingredients except the Parmesan and brush all over the surface of the dough.

⑥ Place on a lightly greased baking (cookie) tray sheet and sprinkle with the Parmesan.

⑦ Cover with lightly greased clingfilm (plastic wrap) and leave in a warm place to prove for about 30 minutes.

⑧ Cook in a preheated oven at 200°C/400°F/gas mark 6 (fan oven 180°C) for 15–25 minutes until golden brown.

DOUGH SETTING
PLUS 1 HOUR SHAPING, RISING AND BAKING

Fast ham and chutney bread
MAKES 1 MEDIUM LOAF

This bread is made using the RAPID cycle, which many breadmakers have. It is important to use fast-acting yeast and warm (30–35°C/85–95°F) water for the bread to be successful.

275 ml/9 fl oz/generous 1 cup warm water
45 ml/3 tbsp sunflower oil
90 ml/6 tbsp chutney
8 small slices of ham, chopped
30 ml/2 tbsp dried milk powder (non-fat dry milk)
5 ml/1 tsp salt
10 ml/2 tsp sugar
225 g/8 oz/2 cups strong white bread flour
100 g/4 oz/1 cup strong wholemeal bread flour
7.5 ml/1½ tsp fast-acting yeast

① Place all the ingredients in the bread pan in the order listed. Place the pan in the breadmaker, ensuring that it is locked into position.

② Close the lid, select the RAPID setting and press START.

③ When the cycle is complete, carefully remove the pan using oven gloves.

④ Tip the loaf out on to a cooling rack and allow to cool before slicing.

RAPID SETTING

Creamy garlic mushroom pockets
MAKES 8

Eat these tasty bread pockets warm for supper or lunch, but be careful that the filling doesn't burst out on you!

For the dough:
275 ml/9 fl oz/generous 1 cup water
30 ml/2 tbsp dried milk powder (non-fat dry milk)
20 ml/1½ tbsp caster (superfine) sugar
5 ml/1 tsp salt
40 ml/2½ tbsp sunflower oil
350 g/12 oz/3 cups strong white bread flour
6 ml/1¼ tsp traditional active dried yeast
For the filling:
2 × 200 g/2 × 7 oz/2 small cans of creamed mushrooms
2 garlic cloves, crushed
Plain (all-purpose) flour, for dusting

① To make the dough, place all the ingredients in the bread pan in the order listed. Place the pan in the breadmaker, ensuring that it is locked into position.

② Close the lid, select the DOUGH setting and press START.

③ When the cycle is complete, carefully remove the pan and tip the dough out on to a lightly floured work surface.

④ Knock back the dough, then divide into eight equal-sized balls. Roll out the balls to flat ovals.

⑤ To make the filling, combine the mushrooms and garlic. Divide the mixture between the ovals, spooning it on to the centres.

⑥ Brush around the dough edges with water, then fold the ovals in half and pinch around the edges to seal.

⑦ Lightly dust with flour and place on a lightly greased baking (cookie) sheet.

⑧ Cover with lightly greased clingfilm (plastic wrap) and leave in a warm place to prove for about 15–20 minutes.

⑨ Bake in a preheated oven at 200°C/400°F/gas mark 6 (fan oven 180°C) for about 15 minutes.

⑩ Eat warm but not hot because of the heat of the filling.

DOUGH SETTING
PLUS 45 MINUTES SHAPING, RISING AND BAKING

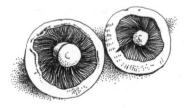

Satay pinwheels
MAKES 20–30

These are a great addition to the buffet table at parties. Eat warm or cold.

For the dough:
275 ml/9 fl oz/generous 1 cup water
30 ml/2 tbsp dried milk powder (non-fat dry milk)
20 ml/1½ tbsp caster (superfine) sugar
5 ml/1 tsp salt
40 ml/2½ tbsp sunflower oil
350 g/12 oz/3 cups strong white bread flour
6 ml/1¼ tsp traditional active dried yeast
For the filling:
45 ml/3 tbsp peanut butter
1 green chilli, seeded and finely chopped
15 ml/1 tbsp tomato purée (paste)
15 ml/1 tbsp soy sauce

① To make the dough, place all the ingredients in the bread pan in the order listed. Place the pan in the breadmaker, ensuring that it is locked into position.

② Close the lid, select the DOUGH setting and press START.

③ When the cycle is complete, carefully remove the pan and tip the dough out on to a lightly floured work surface.

④ Knock back the dough, then roll out to a little larger than a sheet of A4 paper.

⑤ To make the filling, combine all the ingredients and spread all over the surface of the dough.

⑥ Roll up along the long edge and, using a sharp knife, cut the roll into thin slices.

⑦ Place each slice flat-side down on a lightly greased baking (cookie) sheet.

⑧ Cover with lightly greased clingfilm (plastic wrap) and leave in a warm place to prove for about 20 minutes.

⑨ Bake in a preheated oven at 200°C/400°F/gas mark 6 (fan oven 180°C) for about 10–15 minutes.

DOUGH SETTING
PLUS 45 MINUTES SHAPING, RISING AND BAKING

Sun-dried pepper and basil bread
MAKES 1 LARGE LOAF

The sun-dried peppers make this a very 'punchy' bread. It is best eaten with a selection of cheeses and cold meats.

150 ml/¼ pt/⅔ cup water
15 ml/1 tbsp milk
7.5 ml/1½ tsp caster (superfine) sugar
7.5 ml/1½ tsp salt
2.5 ml/½ tsp black pepper
45 ml/3 tbsp olive oil
50 g/2 oz sun-dried peppers
A good handful of fresh basil leaves (or 15 ml/3 tsp dried)
450 g/1 lb/4 cups strong white bread flour
5 ml/1 tsp traditional active dried yeast

① Place the ingredients in the bread pan in the order listed. Place the pan in the breadmaker, ensuring that it is locked into position.

② Close the lid, select the FRENCH setting if you have it or otherwise the BASIC setting and press START.

③ When the cycle is complete, carefully remove the pan using oven gloves.

④ Tip the loaf out on to a cooling rack and allow to cool before slicing.

FRENCH OR BASIC SETTING

Smoked sausage and cheese parcels
MAKES 8–10

Lovely for tea or as part of a party spread!

For the dough:
250 ml/8 fl oz/1 cup water
30 ml/2 tbsp olive oil
15 ml/1 tbsp dried milk powder (non-fat dry milk)
7.5 ml/1½ tsp salt
30 ml/2 tbsp sugar
450 g/1 lb/4 cups strong white bread flour
10 ml/2 tsp traditional active dried yeast
For the filling:
225 g/8 oz/2 cups strong Cheddar cheese, grated
1 smoked sausage ring, sliced

① To make the dough, place all the ingredients in the pan in the order listed. Place the pan in the breadmaker, ensuring that it is locked into position.

② Close the lid, select the DOUGH setting and press START.

③ When the cycle is complete, carefully remove the pan and tip the dough out on to a lightly floured work surface.

④ Knock back the dough, then divide into 8–10 equal-sized pieces. Roll out each piece to a rectangle.

⑤ To make the filling, sprinkle half the cheese over the rectangles, then fold each in half and re-roll to give ovals.

⑥ Divide the sausage slices between the ovals, placing them on the centres. Sprinkle with the remaining cheese.

⑦ Brush around the edges of the ovals with a little water, then bring one end of the oval up, then the other and pinch together to seal.

⑧ Place on an oiled baking (cookie) tray sheet. Cover with lightly greased clingfilm (plastic wrap) and leave in a warm place to prove for 15 minutes.

⑨ Bake in a preheated oven at 200°C/400°F/gas mark 6 (fan oven 180°C) for 15 minutes.

DOUGH SETTING
PLUS 40 MINUTES SHAPING, RISING AND BAKING

Sage and crispy bacon loaf
MAKES 1 LARGE LOAF

Lovely with cheese, salad or poached fish.

300 ml/½ pt/1¼ cups warm water
15 ml/1 tbsp butter
A good handful of fresh sage leaves
8 streaky bacon rashers (slices), grilled (broiled) and chopped
7.5 ml/1½ tsp salt
1.5 ml/¼ tsp freshly ground black pepper
10 ml/2 tsp sugar
250 g/9 oz/2¼ cups strong white bread flour
250 g/9 oz/2¼ cups strong wholemeal bread flour
5 ml/1 tsp traditional active dried yeast

① Place all the ingredients in the bread pan in the order listed. Place the pan in the breadmaker, ensuring that it is locked into position.

② Close the lid, select the WHOLEMEAL setting and press START.

③ When the cycle is complete, carefully remove the pan using oven gloves.

④ Tip the loaf out on to a cooling rack and allow to cool before slicing.

WHOLEMEAL SETTING

Smoked salmon platter
MAKES 1 LARGE LOAF

Eat large wedges of this with a tomato and basil salad or cut into smaller pieces for a party buffet.

For the dough:
300 ml/½ pt/1¼ cups water
45 ml/3 tbsp olive oil
7.5 ml/1½ tsp salt
7.5 ml/1½ tsp sugar
450 g/1 lb/4 cups strong white bread flour
10 ml/2 tsp traditional active dried yeast
For the topping:
30 ml/2 tbsp tomato purée (paste)
1 large red onion, sliced
1 courgette (zucchini), sliced
1 large tomato, sliced
175 g/6 oz smoked salmon, cut into ribbons
A good handful of fresh basil leaves, torn
100 g/4 oz/1 cup Mozzarella cheese, grated
Coarse salt and freshly ground black pepper

① To make the dough, place all the ingredients in the bread pan in the order listed. Place the pan in the breadmaker, ensuring, that it is locked into position.

② Close the lid, select the DOUGH setting and press START.

③ When the cycle is complete, carefully remove the pan and tip the dough out on to a lightly floured work surface. Knock back the dough, then roll out to line a 30 × 20 cm/ 12 × 8 in baking (cookie) sheet.

④ To make the topping, spread the tomato purée over the dough, then arrange the remaining ingredients over, finishing with the Mozzarella and seasoning.

⑤ Cover with lightly greased clingfilm (plastic wrap) and leave in a warm place to prove for 10 minutes, then bake in a preheated oven at 220°C/425°F/gas mark 7 (fan oven 200°C) for 15 minutes.

DOUGH SETTING
PLUS 45 MINUTES SHAPING, RISING AND BAKING

Garlic and oregano bread
MAKES 1 LARGE LOAF

This is a very garlicky bread that makes a wonderful accompaniment to soups, stews and steak.

200 ml/7 fl oz/scant 1 cup water
7.5 ml/1½ tsp salt
30 ml/2 tbsp olive oil
450 g/1 lb/4 cups strong white bread flour
A good handful of fresh oregano leaves (or 15–20 ml/ 3–4 tsp dried)
4 large garlic cloves, crushed
5 ml/1 tsp traditional active dried yeast

① Place the ingredients in the bread pan in the order listed. Place the pan in the breadmaker, ensuring that it is locked into position.

② Close the lid, select the FRENCH setting if you have it or otherwise the BASIC setting and press START.

③ When the cycle is complete, carefully remove the pan using oven gloves.

④ Tip the loaf out on to a cooling rack and allow to cool before slicing.

FRENCH OR BASIC SETTING

Potato and goats' cheese bread
MAKES 1 LARGE LOAF

Try this one warm with grilled (broiled) meat or fish or a fresh tomato salad.

275 ml/9 fl oz/generous 1 cup water
1 egg
175 g/6 oz/1 cup cold mashed potato
175 g/6 oz/1½ cups hard goats' cheese, grated
20 ml/1½ tbsp sunflower oil
45 ml/3 tbsp dried milk powder (non-fat dry milk)
5 ml/1 tsp salt
2.5 ml/½ tsp freshly ground black pepper
15 ml/1 tbsp sugar
400 g/14 oz/3½ cups strong white bread flour
10 ml/2 tsp traditional active dried yeast

① Place all the ingredients in the bread pan in the order listed. Place the pan in the breadmaker, ensuring that it is locked into position.

② Close the lid, select the BASIC setting and press START.

③ When the cycle is complete, carefully remove the pan using oven gloves.

④ Tip the loaf out on to a cooling rack and allow to cool before slicing.

BASIC SETTING

Continental and foreign breads

*T*his chapter deals with some exciting breads from around the world and demonstrates how easy it is to get tasty and authentic results using the breadmaker. These breads make ideal accompaniments to foreign and exotic meals.

Bagels
MAKES 10

These Jewish yeast rolls are a bit time-consuming to make, but are well worth the effort. They are best eaten fresh from the oven or split and toasted – they tend to toughen as they cool and become chewy.

For the dough:
275 ml/9 fl oz/generous 1 cup water
20 ml/1½ tbsp caster (superfine) sugar
5 ml/1 tsp salt
350 g/12 oz/3 cups strong white bread flour
6 ml/1¼ tsp traditional active dried yeast
A little oil
15 ml/1 tbsp granulated sugar
A little oatmeal
For the glaze:
1 egg, beaten
10 ml/2 tsp water

① To make the dough, place all the ingredients except the oil, granulated sugar and oatmeal in the bread pan in the order listed. Place the pan in the breadmaker, ensuring that it is locked into position.

② Close the lid, select the DOUGH setting (or use the BAGEL setting if your model has one) and press START.

③ When the cycle is complete, carefully remove the pan and tip the dough out on to a lightly floured work surface.

④ Knock back the dough and divide into 10 equal-sized pieces. Roll into smooth balls, then, using the thumbs, make a large hole in the middle of each to give a ring doughnut shape.

⑤ Place on a lightly greased baking (cookie) sheet and brush the top of each bagel with a little oil.

⑥ Cover loosely with clingfilm (plastic wrap) and a dry tea towel (dish cloth), then leave in a warm place to prove for about 30 minutes.

⑦ Meanwhile, bring a large saucepan of water (about 1.5 litres/2½ pt/6 cups) to the boil with the granulated sugar.

⑧ After proving, drop three or four of the bagels at a time into the saucepan and simmer for about 2 minutes, turning once.

⑨ Remove with a draining spoon and place on kitchen paper (paper towels).

⑩ Place on a greased baking (cookie) sheet dusted with a little oatmeal.

⑪ To make the glaze, mix together the egg and water and brush over the tops of the bagels.

⑫ Bake in a preheated oven at 220°C/425°F/gas mark 7 (fan oven 200°C) for 15 minutes.

DOUGH OR BAGEL SETTING
PLUS 1¼ HOURS SHAPING, RISING AND BAKING

Variations

Onion bagels: follow the recipe as above, but add a small chopped onion to the breadmaker at the beginning of the DOUGH cycle and sprinkle with dried onion flakes before baking.

Cheese and herb bagels: follow the recipe as above, but add either 30 ml/2 tbsp of chopped mixed fresh herbs or 10 ml/2 tsp of mixed dried herbs to the breadmaker at the beginning of the DOUGH cycle. Sprinkle with finely grated full-flavoured cheese before baking.

Fried bread

MAKES 8

An Indian-style bread that lends itself well to curries and spicy dishes.

275 ml/9 fl oz/generous 1 cup water
40 ml/2½ tbsp olive oil
30 ml/2 tbsp dried milk powder (non-fat dry milk)
20 ml/1½ tbsp honey
5 ml/1 tsp salt
100 g/4 oz/1 cup strong white bread flour
100 g/4 oz/1 cup spelt flour
100 g/4 oz/1 cup strong wholemeal bread flour
7.5 ml/1½ tsp traditional active dried yeast
Oil, for shallow-frying

① Place all the ingredients in the bread pan in the order listed. Place the pan in the breadmaker, ensuring that it is locked into position.

② Close the lid, select the DOUGH setting and press START.

③ When the cycle is complete, carefully remove the pan and tip the dough out on to a lightly floured work surface.

④ Knock back the dough, then divide into eight equal-sized pieces. Roll them out to give very flat ovals.

⑤ Cover loosely with clingfilm (plastic wrap) and leave in a warm place to prove for about 10 minutes.

⑥ Heat about 30 ml/2 tbsp of oil in a frying pan (skillet) and fry (sauté) the ovals a few at a time for about 3 minutes on each side.

⑦ Drain on kitchen paper (paper towels) and eat while still warm.

DOUGH SETTING
PLUS 25 MINUTES SHAPING, RISING AND COOKING

Grissini
MAKES 25

These Italian-style bread sticks are brilliant for munching on when you're peckish, as well as for serving with dips.

For the dough:
275 ml/9 fl oz/generous 1 cup water
40 ml/2½ tbsp olive oil
30 ml/2 tbsp dried milk powder (non-fat dry milk)
20 ml/1½ tbsp honey
5 ml/1 tsp salt
100 g/4 oz/1 cup strong white bread flour
100 g/4 oz/1 cup spelt flour
100 g/4 oz/1 cup strong wholemeal bread flour
7.5 ml/1½ tsp traditional active dried yeast
For the topping:
A little milk
Coarse salt
Sesame seeds

① Place all the ingredients in the bread pan in the order listed. Place the pan in the breadmaker, ensuring that it is locked into position.

② Close the lid, select the DOUGH setting and press START. When the cycle is complete, carefully remove the pan and tip the dough out on to a lightly floured work surface.

③ Knock back the dough, then divide into 25 equal-sized pieces. Roll each into a long stick about 30 cm/12 in long. Brush each stick with milk, then sprinkle with either salt or sesame seeds.

④ Place on a lightly greased baking (cookie) sheet. Cover loosely with lightly greased clingfilm (plastic wrap) and leave in a warm place to prove for about 10 minutes.

⑤ Bake in a preheated oven at 220°C/425°F/gas mark 7 (fan oven 200°C) for about 5–10 minutes until golden.

DOUGH SETTING
PLUS 30 MINUTES SHAPING, RISING AND BAKING

Farmhouse cider and strong cheese baguettes

MAKES 2

These full-flavoured baguettes really round off a simple salad. Alternatively, fill with smoked ham.

For the dough:
300 ml/½ pt/1¼ cups strong cider
100 g/4 oz/1 cup strong farmhouse Cheddar cheese, grated
7.5 ml/1½ tsp salt
7.5 ml/1½ tsp sugar
15 g/½ oz/1 tbsp margarine
450 g/1 lb/4 cups strong white bread flour
7.5 ml/1½ tsp traditional active dried yeast
For the glaze:
1 egg yolk
25 g/1 oz/¼ cup Cheddar cheese, grated

① To make the dough, place all the ingredients in the bread pan in the order listed. Place the pan in the breadmaker, ensuring that it is locked into position.

② Close the lid, select the DOUGH setting and press START.

③ When the cycle is complete, carefully remove the pan and tip out the dough.

④ Knock back the dough, divide in half and shape into two baguettes each about 30 cm/12 in long. Make diagonal slashes on the surface of each using a sharp knife.

⑤ Place on a lightly greased baking (cookie) sheet.

⑥ To make the glaze, mix the egg yolk with a little water and brush over the surface of the dough. Sprinkle the cheese over.

⑦ Cover loosely with clingfilm (plastic wrap) and leave in a warm place to prove for about 30–40 minutes until doubled in size.

⑧ Bake in a preheated oven at 190°C/375°F/gas mark 5 (fan oven 170°C) for 15–25 minutes until golden brown.

⑨ Cool slightly before eating, though these are definitely best eaten warm.

DOUGH SETTING
PLUS 1¼ HOURS SHAPING, RISING AND BAKING

Tikka and coriander corn loaf
MAKES 1 MEDIUM LOAF

A close-textured, full-flavoured bread. Use to mop up casseroles and stews.

375 ml/13 fl oz/1½ cups water
20 ml/2½ tbsp sunflower oil
45 ml/3 tbsp tikka paste
30 ml/2 tbsp chopped fresh coriander (cilantro)
5 ml/1 tsp salt
5 ml/1 tsp sugar
275 g/10 oz/2½ cups strong white bread flour
75 g/3 oz/¾ cup cornmeal
7.5 ml/1½ tsp traditional active dried yeast

① Place all the ingredients in the bread pan in the order listed. Place the pan in the breadmaker, ensuring that it is locked into position.

② Close the lid, select the BASIC setting and press START.

③ When the cycle is complete, carefully remove the pan using oven gloves.

④ Tip the loaf out on to a cooling rack and allow to cool before slicing.

BASIC SETTING

Pesto and Brie Italian flat breads
MAKES 6

Enjoy warm or cold with seafood, salads and soups

For the dough:
350 ml/12 fl oz/1⅓ cups water
10 ml/2 tsp honey
5 ml/1 tsp salt
30 ml/2 tbsp olive oil
450 g/1 lb/4 cups strong white bread flour
10 ml/2 tsp traditional active dried yeast
For the topping:
90 ml/6 tbsp red pesto
175 g/6 oz Brie, thinly sliced

① To make the dough, place all the ingredients in the bread pan in the order listed. Place the pan in the breadmaker, ensuring that it is locked into position.

② Close the lid, select the DOUGH setting and press START.

③ When the cycle is complete, carefully remove the pan and tip the dough out on to a lightly floured work surface.

④ Knock back the dough, divide into six equal-sized pieces and roll into balls.

⑤ Roll each dough ball out to a flat oval, then place on a lightly greased baking (cookie) sheet.

⑥ Spread the surface of each with the pesto, then top with the Brie.

⑦ Cover with lightly greased clingfilm (plastic wrap) and leave in a warm place to prove for about 30 minutes.

⑧ Bake in a preheated oven at 200°C/400°F/gas mark 6 (fan oven 180°C) for about 10–15 minutes.

DOUGH SETTING
PLUS 50 MINUTES SHAPING, RISING AND BAKING

Madras flat bread
MAKES 4

Spicy little pitta-type breads that can be split and filled with salad, kebabs or your favourite filling.

For the dough:
275 ml/9 fl oz/generous 1 cup water
60 ml/4 tbsp Madras curry powder
30 ml/2 tbsp dried milk powder (non-fat dry milk)
20 ml/1½ tbsp caster (superfine) sugar
5 ml/1 tsp salt
30 ml/2 tbsp sunflower oil
350 g/12 oz/3 cups strong white bread flour
6 ml/1¼ tsp traditional active dried yeast
For the topping:
30 ml/2 tbsp Madras curry paste

① To make the dough, place all the ingredients in the bread pan in the order listed. Place the pan in the breadmaker, ensuring that it is locked into position.

② Close the lid, select the DOUGH setting and press START.

③ When the cycle is complete, carefully remove the pan and tip the dough out on to a lightly floured work surface.

④ Knock back the dough, then divide into four equal-sized balls. Flatten each out to an oval.

⑤ Spread the curry paste all over the surface of the dough.

⑥ Place on a lightly greased baking (cookie) sheet, cover with lightly greased clingfilm (plastic wrap) and leave in a warm place to prove for about 20 minutes.

⑦ Bake in a preheated oven at 200°C/400°F/gas mark 6 (fan oven 180°C) for about 15 minutes.

DOUGH SETTING
PLUS 45 MINUTES SHAPING, RISING AND BAKING

Aubergine and anchovy focaccia
MAKES 1 LARGE LOAF

The aubergine (eggplant) and anchovy make this a very moist, flavoursome bread, which goes well with lamb and beef stews or rich vegetable soups.

50 g/2 oz packet sun-dried aubergines
7.5 ml/1½ tsp salt
30 ml/2 tbsp olive oil
450 g/1 lb/4 cups strong white bread flour
7.5 ml/1½ tsp traditional active dried yeast
50 g/2 oz/1 very small can of anchovies, drained and oil reserved
A little cornmeal, for sprinkling
A little coarse salt, for sprinkling

① Rehydrate the aubergines according to the packet instructions and reserve the soaking liquid.

② Make the soaking liquid up to 250 ml/8 fl oz/1 cup with cold water. Place in the bread pan and add the remaining ingredients except the aubergines and anchovies in the order listed.

③ Place the pan in the breadmaker, ensuring that it is locked into position.

④ Close the lid, select the DOUGH setting and press START.

⑤ Add the aubergines and anchovies at the buzzer or after the first kneading.

⑥ When the cycle is complete, carefully remove the pan and tip the dough on to a lightly floured work surface.

⑦ Knock back the dough. Sprinkle a little cornmeal in the bottom of a 28 × 40 cm/11 × 16 in baking tin (pan), then press the dough out to fill the pan.

⑧ Cover loosely with clingfilm (plastic wrap) and leave in a warm place to prove for 5 minutes.

⑨ Press your fingers into the dough to make deep holes in the surface. Drizzle the reserved anchovy oil over the surface and sprinkle with coarse salt.

⑩ Bake in a preheated oven to 200°C/400°F/gas mark 6 (fan oven 180°C) for about 15 minutes until golden.

DOUGH SETTING
PLUS 25 MINUTES SHAPING, RISING AND BAKING

Dark pumpernickel
MAKES 1 MEDIUM LOAF

A close-textured bread, which is excellent with a range of continental cheeses and cold meats.

150 ml/¼ pt/⅔ cup water
15 ml/1 tbsp sunflower oil
30 ml/2 tbsp black treacle (molasses)
5 ml/1 tsp salt
45 ml/3 tbsp dried milk powder (non-fat dry milk)
300 g/11 oz/2¾ cups strong white bread flour
25 g/1 oz/¼ cup cornflour (cornstarch)
100 g/4 oz/1 cup rye flour
7.5 ml/1½ tsp traditional active dried yeast

① Place all the ingredients in the bread pan in the order listed. Place the pan in the breadmaker, ensuring that it is locked into position.

② Close the lid, select the WHOLEMEAL setting and press START.

③ When the cycle is complete, carefully remove the pan using oven gloves.

④ Tip the loaf out on to a cooling rack and allow to cool before slicing.

WHOLEMEAL SETTING

Brioche

MAKES 1 SMALL LOAF

This is a wonderful breakfast bread, which can be dunked into your coffee. Alternatively, make up your own syrup, with or without alcohol, and use this bread to mop it up.

120 ml/4 fl oz/½ cup water
2 eggs
2.5 ml/½ tsp salt
45 ml/3 tbsp sugar
225 g/8 oz/2 cups strong white bread flour
5 ml/1 tsp traditional active dried yeast
120 g/4½ oz/generous ½ cup butter, softened

① Place all the ingredients except the butter in the bread pan in the order listed. Place the pan in the breadmaker, ensuring that it is locked into position.

② Close the lid, select the BASIC setting and press START.

③ Start adding the butter about 5 minutes into the kneading process, adding 15 ml/1 tbsp at a time and giving it a chance to mix in. Close the lid.

④ When the cycle is complete, switch off the machine, open the lid and allow the loaf to cool inside for about 30 minutes.

⑤ Carefully remove the pan using oven gloves.

⑥ Tip the loaf out on to a cooling rack and allow to cool before slicing.

BASIC SETTING

Olive and chilli pitta bread
MAKES 12

These full-flavoured pitta breads make a wonderful lunch when filled with Feta cheese and crisp lettuce or slices of ripe tomato and cold cooked meat. Eat them warm or cold.

300 ml/½ pt/1¼ cups water
7.5 ml/1½ tsp salt
7.5 ml/1½ tsp sugar
20 ml/1½ tbsp olive oil
1 red chilli, seeded and halved
1 green chilli, seeded and halved
450 g/1 lb/4 cups strong white bread flour
7.5 ml/1½ tsp traditional active dried yeast
100 g/4 oz mixed stoned (pitted) olives

① Place all the ingredients except the olives in the bread pan in the order listed. Place the pan in the breadmaker, ensuring that it is locked into position.

② Close the lid, select the DOUGH setting and press START.

③ Add the olives at the buzzer or after the first kneading.

④ When the cycle is complete, carefully remove the pan and tip the dough out on to a lightly floured work surface.

⑤ Knock back the dough, divide into 12 equal-sized pieces and roll into balls. Roll each out to a flat oval and place on a lightly greased baking (cookie) sheet.

⑥ Cover with lightly greased clingfilm (plastic wrap) and leave in a warm place to prove for about 30 minutes.

⑦ Bake in a preheated oven at 200°C/400°F/gas mark 6 (fan oven 180°C) for about 10–15 minutes.

DOUGH SETTING
PLUS 55 MINUTES SHAPING, RISING AND BAKING

Basic pizza dough
MAKES 1 LARGE PIZZA BASE

Use this recipe to make the pizza dough, then shape and top it how you choose. The two recipes that follow give some ideas.

250 ml/8 fl oz/1 cup water
30 ml/2 tbsp olive oil
15 ml/1 tbsp dried milk powder (non-fat dry milk)
7.5 ml/1½ tsp salt
30 ml/2 tbsp sugar
450 g/1 lb/4 cups strong white bread flour
10 ml/2 tsp traditional active dried yeast

① Place all the ingredients in the bread pan in the order listed. Place the pan in the breadmaker, ensuring that it is locked into position.

② Close the lid, select the DOUGH setting and press START.

③ When the cycle is complete, carefully remove the pan and tip the dough out on to a lightly floured work surface.

④ Knock back the dough and roll out to the required shape.

⑤ Place on an oiled baking (cookie) sheet, cover with lightly greased clingfilm (plastic wrap) and leave in a warm place to prove for 15 minutes.

⑥ Top with your chosen ingredients and leave to rest for a further 15 minutes.

⑦ Bake in a preheated oven at 200°C/400°F/gas mark 6 (fan oven 180°C) for 10–15 minutes.

DOUGH SETTING
PLUS 55 MINUTES SHAPING, RISING AND BAKING

fennel and smoked salmon pizza
MAKES 1 LARGE PIZZA

1 large red onion, thinly sliced
1 medium fennel bulb, sliced
5 ml/1 tsp olive oil
1 prepared uncooked pizza base
60 ml/4 tbsp wholegrain mustard
175 g/6 oz smoked salmon, cut into ribbons
175 g/6 oz/1½ cups Mozzarella cheese, grated

① Put the onion, fennel and oil in a lidded saucepan and cook over a moderate heat for 10–15 minutes until very soft.

② Spread the pizza base with the mustard, top with the onion and fennel mixture and arrange the salmon ribbons over the top. Sprinkle the Mozzarella over. Leave to rest for 15 minutes.

③ Bake in a preheated oven at 200°C/400°F/gas mark 6 (fan oven 180°C) for about 15 minutes.

DOUGH SETTING FOR PIZZA BASE
PLUS 45 MINUTES PREPARATION AND BAKING

Red pesto and artichoke pizza
MAKES 1 LARGE PIZZA

1 prepared uncooked pizza base
90 ml/6 tbsp red pesto
400 g/14 oz/1 large can of artichoke hearts, drained and sliced
175 g/6 oz/1½ cups Mozzarella cheese, grated

① Spread the pizza base with the pesto, top with the artichoke hearts and sprinkle the Mozzarella over. Leave to rest for 15 minutes.

② Bake in a preheated oven at 200°C/400°F/gas mark 6 (fan oven 180°C) for about 15 minutes.

DOUGH SETTING FOR PIZZA BASE
PLUS 30 MINUTES PREPARATION AND BAKING

Croissants

MAKES 8 LARGE CROISSANTS

It takes time to get perfect croissants, but using the breadmaker does take the strain out of the mixing and kneading and helps to ensure good results every time.

375 ml/13 fl oz/1½ cups water
60 ml/4 tbsp dried milk powder (non-fat dry milk)
60 ml/4 tbsp sugar
10 ml/2 tsp salt
60 ml/4 tbsp sunflower oil
450 g/1 lb/4 cups strong white bread flour
10 ml/2 tsp traditional dried yeast
225 g/8 oz/1 cup butter, chilled
1 egg, beaten
10 ml/2 tsp water

① Place all the ingredients except the butter, egg and water in the bread pan in the order listed. Place the pan in the breadmaker, ensuring that it is locked into position.

② Close the lid, select the DOUGH setting and press START.

③ Meanwhile, place the butter between two sheets of greaseproof (waxed) paper and roll out to a 23 cm/9 in square. Return to the fridge.

④ When the cycle is complete, carefully remove the pan and tip the dough out on to a lightly floured work surface.

⑤ Knock back the dough, then roll out to a 30 cm/12 in square. Arrange the butter diagonally across the centre of the dough and bring the corners of the dough to meet in the middle so that all the butter is covered.

⑥ Put the dough into the freezer for 5 minutes, then roll it out to a 50 × 25 cm /20 × 10 in rectangle. Fold in both ends to meet in the middle, then fold one half over the other. Return to the freezer for 15 minutes.

⑦ Repeat the rolling and folding process with the rested dough, then return to the freezer for a further 15 minutes.

⑧ Finally, roll the rested dough out to a 12.5 cm/5 in wide strip. Cut the strip into 12.5 cm/5 in squares, then cut each in half diagonally to give triangles. Roll out each to stretch it by about a third.

⑨ Mix together the egg and water and use to brush over each triangle. Roll up the dough from the wide base and coil the ends round to form crescents.

⑩ Brush the surface with egg wash, the leave in a warm place to prove for a further 20 minutes.

⑪ Bake at 220°C/425°F/gas mark 7 (fan oven 200°C) for 10–15 minutes until golden and puffy. Eat warm or cold.

DOUGH SETTING
PLUS 1½ HOURS SHAPING, RISING AND BAKING

Variations

Cheese and ham croissants: follow the recipe as above, but at step 9 lay a slice of ham then a slice of cheese on the dough triangle before rolling up.

Salami and Brie croissants: follow the recipe as above, but at step 9 lay a slice of salami, then a slice of Brie, then 2 basil leaves on each dough triangle before rolling up.

Chinese-style dumplings
MAKES ABOUT 18

These won tons take a little time to prepare, but are well worth the effort! Experiment with your own fillings and serve with traditional Chinese dipping sauces.

For the dough:
275 ml/9 fl oz/generous 1 cup water
30 ml/2 tbsp dried milk powder (non-fat dry milk)
20 ml/1½ tbsp caster (superfine) sugar
5 ml/1 tsp salt
40 ml/2½ tbsp sunflower oil
350 g/12 oz/3 cups strong white bread flour
6 ml/1¼ tsp traditional active dried yeast
For the filling:
350 g/12 oz minced pork or chicken
1 red onion, finely chopped
4 small mushrooms, chopped
1 garlic clove, crushed
15 ml/1 tbsp soy sauce
2.5 ml/½ tsp Chinese five-spice powder
30 ml/2 tbsp chopped fresh lemon grass
Salt and freshly ground black pepper
A little oil, for greasing

① To make the dough, place all the ingredients in the bread pan in the order listed. Place the pan in the breadmaker, ensuring that it is locked into position.

② Close the lid, select the DOUGH setting and press START.

③ Meanwhile, mix together all the filling ingredients.

④ When the cycle is complete, carefully remove the pan and tip the dough out on to a lightly floured work surface.

⑤ Knock back the dough and divide into about 18 equal-sized portions. Shape into smooth balls, then roll out each to a 13 cm/5 in diameter round.

⑥ Divide the filling between the rounds, spooning it into the centre. Pull the dough up around the edges and pinch together to seal and form pouch shapes.

⑦ Place on a lightly greased baking (cookie) sheet with the pleated side down.

⑧ Cover loosely with clingfilm (plastic wrap) and leave in a warm place to prove for about 30 minutes.

⑨ Invert the dumplings and place on a lightly greased heatproof plate or flat dish. Place in a bamboo steamer or stand the plate on a flan tin (pie pan) in a wok or large frying pan (skillet) so that the steam comes up around the sides of the plate.

⑩ Cover the steamer and steam the dumplings over boiling water for about 25 minutes.

DOUGH SETTING
PLUS 1¼ HOURS SHAPING, RISING AND COOKING

Challah bread

MAKES 1 LARGE LOAF

This traditional Jewish bread is best eaten warm.

For the dough:
200 ml/7 fl oz/scant 1 cup water
1 egg
15 ml/1 tbsp kosher margarine
5 ml/1 tsp caster (superfine) sugar
2.5 ml/½ tsp salt
450 g/1 lb/4 cups strong white bread flour
7.5 ml/1½ tsp traditional active dried yeast
For the glaze:
1 egg, beaten
10 ml/2 tsp water

① To make the dough, place the all ingredients in the bread pan in the order listed. Place the pan in the breadmaker, ensuring that it is locked into position.

② Close the lid, select the DOUGH setting and press START.

③ When the cycle is complete, carefully remove the pan and tip the dough out on to a lightly floured work surface.

④ Knock back the dough, then cut off a third and reserve.

⑤ Roll the large piece of dough into a sausage about 30 cm/12 in long. Twist slightly, then place on a lightly greased baking (cookie) sheet. Mix together the egg and water for the glaze and brush over the dough.

⑥ Divide the remaining dough into three pieces and roll each to about the same length as the big sausage. Plait the three pieces, then lay on top of the sausage on the baking sheet. Cover with lightly greased clingfilm (plastic wrap) and leave in a warm place to prove for about 25 minutes.

⑦ Bake in a preheated oven at 200°C/400°F/gas mark 6 (fan oven 180°C) for about 30 minutes.

DOUGH SETTING
PLUS 1¼ HOURS SHAPING, RISING AND BAKING

french bread

MAKES 1 MEDIUM LOAF

Always a popular accompaniment to any meal as well as a must for picnics and buffets.

---

250 ml/8 fl oz/1 cup water
30 ml/2 tbsp dried milk powder (non-fat dry milk)
5 ml/1 tsp salt
15 ml/1 tbsp sugar
350 g/12 oz/3 cups strong white bread flour
5 ml/1 tsp traditional active dried yeast

---

① Place all the ingredients in the bread pan in the order listed. Place the pan in the breadmaker, ensuring that it is locked into position.

② Close the lid, select the FRENCH setting and press START.

③ When the cycle is complete, carefully remove the pan using oven gloves.

④ Tip the loaf out on to a cooling rack and allow to cool before slicing.

FRENCH SETTING .

French stick
MAKES 1 MEDIUM LOAF

It's worth making some soup as an excuse to eat this bread! Baguettes use the same dough and are given as a variation below.

250 ml/8 fl oz/1 cup water
30 ml/2 tbsp dried milk powder (non-fat dry milk)
5 ml/1 tsp salt
15 ml/1 tbsp sugar
350 g/12 oz/3 cups strong white bread flour
5 ml/1 tsp traditional active dried yeast

① Place all the ingredients in the bread pan in the order listed. Place the pan in the breadmaker, ensuring that it is locked into position.

② Close the lid, select the DOUGH setting and press START.

③ When the cycle is complete, carefully remove the pan and tip the dough out on to a lightly floured work surface.

④ Knock back the dough, then roll into a long stick.

⑤ Place on a lightly greased baking (cookie) sheet. Cover loosely with lightly greased clingfilm (plastic wrap) and leave in a warm place to prove for 20–30 minutes.

⑥ Bake in a preheated oven at 220°C/425°F/gas mark 7 (fan oven 200°C) for about 20 minutes.

DOUGH SETTING
PLUS 50 MINUTES SHAPING, RISING AND BAKING

Variation

Baguettes: follow the recipe as above, but at step 4 shape into about six equal-sized portions and roll into long torpedo shapes. When cooled, split and butter and fill with cold meat or cheese and salad.

Rolls and buns

*M*ost of the bread recipes in this book can be adjusted to make rolls, but this chapter concentrates on rolls and buns and explains the techniques of shaping. You can also ring the changes by experimenting with different glazes and toppings:

Suggested glazes: oil, melted butter, egg (1 yolk beaten with 10 ml/2 tsp water), milk, salt (5 ml/1 tsp mixed with 30 ml/ 2 tbsp water).

Suggested toppings: sunflower seeds, poppy seeds, sesame seeds, rolled oats, crushed peanuts, cracked wheat, grated or crumbled cheese, a sprinkling of dried herbs.

White bread rolls
MAKES 8–12

Use this basic bread roll recipe to create your favourite shapes.

---

275 ml/9 fl oz/generous 1 cup water
30 ml/2 tbsp dried milk powder (non-fat dry milk)
20 ml/1½ tbsp caster (superfine) sugar
5 ml/1 tsp salt
40 ml/2½ tbsp sunflower oil
350 g/12 oz/3 cups strong white bread flour
6 ml/1¼ tsp traditional active dried yeast

---

① Place all the ingredients in the bread pan in the order listed. Place the pan in the breadmaker, ensuring that it is locked into position.

② Close the lid, select the DOUGH setting and press START.

③ When the cycle is complete, carefully remove the pan and tip the dough out on to a lightly floured work surface.

④ Knock back the dough, divide into 8–12 equal-sized pieces and shape as you wish.

⑤ Place on a lightly greased baking (cookie) sheet. Cover loosely with clingfilm (plastic wrap) and leave in a warm place to prove for about 30 minutes.

⑥ Bake in a preheated oven at 220°C/425°F/gas mark 7 (fan oven 200°C) for 10–15 minutes depending on size.

DOUGH SETTING
PLUS 50 MINUTES SHAPING, RISING AND BAKING

Wholemeal bread rolls

MAKES 8–12

Use this basic bread roll recipe to create your favourite shapes. I have found that the best results for wholemeal rolls are achieved by using some plain white flour as well. However, if you like them slightly heavier, try using all wholemeal flour.

---

275 ml/9 fl oz/generous 1 cup water
30 ml/2 tbsp dried milk powder (non-fat dry milk)
20 ml/1½ tbsp caster (superfine) sugar
5 ml/1 tsp salt
40 ml/2½ tbsp sunflower oil
100 g/4 oz/1 cup strong white bread flour
225 g/8 oz/2 cups strong wholemeal bread flour
6 ml/1¼ tsp traditional active dried yeast

---

① Place all the ingredients in the bread pan in the order listed. Place the pan in the breadmaker, ensuring that it is locked into position.

② Close the lid, select the DOUGH setting and press START.

③ When the cycle is complete, carefully remove the pan and tip the dough out on to a lightly floured work surface.

④ Knock back the dough, divide into 8–12 equal-sized pieces and shape as you wish.

⑤ Place on a lightly greased baking (cookie) sheet. Cover loosely with clingfilm (plastic wrap) and leave in a warm place to prove for about 30 minutes.

⑥ Bake in a preheated oven at 220°C/425°F/gas mark 7 (fan oven 200°C) for 10–15 minutes depending on size.

DOUGH SETTING
PLUS 50 MINUTES SHAPING, RISING AND BAKING

Breakfast buns
MAKES 6

*These tasty buns are a compact breakfast, best eaten warm
from the oven but also good cold for picnics.*

For the dough:
275 ml/9 fl oz/generous 1 cup water
40 ml/2½ tbsp olive oil
40 ml/2½ tbsp dried milk powder (non-fat dry milk)
40 ml/2½ tbsp sugar
7.5 ml/1½ tsp salt
350 g/12 oz/3 cups strong white bread flour
7.5 ml/1½ tsp traditional active dried yeast
For the filling:
6 smoked bacon rashers (slices)
6 mushrooms, sliced
2 tomatoes, sliced
A little milk, for brushing

① To make the dough, place all the ingredients in the bread
pan in the order listed. Place the pan in the breadmaker,
ensuring that it is locked into position.

② Close the lid, select the DOUGH setting and press START.

③ Meanwhile, to make the filling, heat a frying pan (skillet)
and fry (sauté) the bacon for a few minutes on each side.
Add the mushrooms, then the tomatoes and fry until
cooked. Put to one side to cool.

④ When the cycle is complete, carefully remove the pan and
tip the dough out on to a lightly floured work surface.

⑤ Knock back the dough, then divide into six equal-sized
pieces.

⑥ Flatten each piece, then divide the bacon, mushrooms and
tomatoes between the centres of each, breaking the bacon
a little if necessary.

⑦ Brush round the edges of the dough with a little water, then bring them up around the filling and pinch together to seal.

⑧ Place join-side down on a lightly greased baking (cookie) sheet.

⑨ Cover loosely with lightly greased clingfilm (plastic wrap) and leave in a warm place to prove for about 20 minutes.

⑩ Bake in a preheated oven at 220°C/425°F/gas mark 7 (fan oven 200°C) for about 10–15 minutes.

DOUGH SETTING
PLUS 45 MINUTES SHAPING, RISING AND BAKING

Shrimp knots

MAKES 6

These little rolls have a distinctly Oriental taste. They are a wonderful accompaniment to Chinese soups and noodle dishes.

275 ml/9 fl oz/generous 1 cup water
40 ml/2½ tbsp olive oil
7.5 ml/1½ tsp Chinese shrimp paste
30 ml/2 tbsp chopped lemon grass
40 ml/2½ tbsp dried milk powder (non-fat dry milk)
40 ml/2½ tbsp sugar
7.5 ml/1½ tsp salt
350 g/12 oz/3 cups strong white bread flour
7.5 ml/1½ tsp traditional active dried yeast

① Place all the ingredients in the bread pan in the order listed. Place the pan in the breadmaker, ensuring that it is locked into position.

② Close the lid, select the DOUGH setting and press START.

③ When the cycle is complete, carefully remove the pan and tip the dough out on to a lightly floured work surface.

④ Knock back the dough, then divide into six equal-sized pieces. Roll out each into a long sausage, then form each one into a loose knot.

⑤ Place on a lightly greased baking (cookie) sheet. Cover loosely with lightly greased clingfilm (plastic wrap) and leave in a warm place to prove for about 20 minutes.

⑥ Bake in a preheated oven at 220°C/425°F/gas mark 7 (fan oven 200°C) for about 10–15 minutes.

DOUGH SETTING
PLUS 45 MINUTES SHAPING, RISING AND BAKING

Summer herb and onion rolls

MAKES 10

For the dough:
275 ml/9 fl oz/generous 1 cup water
45 ml/3 tbsp sunflower oil
30 ml/2 tbsp dried milk powder (non-fat dry milk)
10 ml/2 tsp honey
5 ml/1 tsp salt
A large handful of mixed fresh herb leaves, e.g. sage,
    thyme, parsley, rosemary, marjoram
1 shallot, chopped
225 g/8 oz/2 cups strong white bread flour
100 g/4 oz/1 cup strong wholemeal bread flour
6 ml/1¼ tsp traditional active dried yeast
For the glaze:
1 egg, beaten
10 ml/2 tsp water

① To make the dough, place all the ingredients in the bread pan in the order listed. Place the pan in the breadmaker, ensuring that it is locked into position.

② Close the lid, select the DOUGH setting and press START.

③ When the cycle is complete, carefully remove the pan and tip the dough out on to a lightly floured work surface

④ Knock back the dough and divide into 10 equal-sized pieces. Roll each into a smooth ball, then roll and lengthen slightly to form batons.

⑤ Place on a lightly greased baking (cookie) sheet, cover with lightly greased clingfilm (plastic wrap) and leave in a warm place to prove for about 20 minutes.

⑥ To make the glaze, mix together the egg and water and brush all over the rolls. Bake in a preheated oven at 220°C/425°F/gas mark 7 (fan oven 200°C) for about 10–15 minutes. Eat warm or cold.

DOUGH SETTING
PLUS 45 MINUTES SHAPING, RISING AND BAKING

Blue cheese and caraway coils
MAKES 10

Try these warm with fresh vegetable soups.

For the dough:
275 ml/9 fl oz/generous 1 cup water
45 ml/3 tbsp sunflower oil
30 ml/2 tbsp dried milk powder (non-fat dry milk)
7.5 ml/1½ tsp sugar
5 ml/1 tsp salt
100 g/4 oz/1 cup blue cheese, crumbled
45 ml/3 tbsp caraway seeds
350 g/12 oz/3 cups strong white bread flour
6 ml/1¼ tsp traditional active dried yeast
For the glaze and topping:
1 egg, beaten
10 ml/2 tsp water
5 ml/1 tsp caraway seeds

① To make the dough, place all the ingredients in the bread pan in the order listed. Place the pan in the breadmaker, ensuring that it is locked into position.

② Close the lid, select the DOUGH setting and press START.

③ When the cycle is complete, carefully remove the pan and tip the dough out on to a lightly floured work surface.

④ Knock back the dough and divide into 10 equal-sized pieces. Roll each into a smooth ball, then roll into long sausages.

⑤ Wind up each sausage to form a tight coil. Seal the end in place by brushing with a little water.

⑥ Place on a lightly greased baking (cookie) sheet. Cover with lightly greased clingfilm (plastic wrap) and leave in a warm place to prove for about 20 minutes.

⑦ To make the glaze, mix together the egg and water and brush all over the coils. Sprinkle with the caraway seeds.

⑧ Bake in a preheated oven at 220°C/425°F/gas mark 7 (fan oven 200°C) for about 10–15 minutes. Eat warm or cold.

DOUGH SETTING
PLUS 45 MINUTES SHAPING, RISING AND BAKING

Hot cross buns
MAKES 8–10

A traditional Easter favourite made easy with the breadmaker.

For the dough:
150 ml/¼ pt/⅔ cup warm milk
1 egg
30 ml/2 tbsp butter
30 ml/2 tbsp caster (superfine) sugar
2.5 ml/½ tsp salt
350 g/12 oz/3 cups strong white bread flour
5 ml/1 tsp ground cinnamon
2.5 ml/½ tsp mixed (apple-pie) spice
7.5 ml/1½ tsp traditional active dried yeast
100 g/4 oz/⅔ cup dried mixed fruit (fruit cake mix)
For the glaze:
1 egg, beaten
10 ml/2 tsp water

① To make the dough, place all the ingredients except the dried fruit in the bread pan in the order listed. Place the pan in the breadmaker, ensuring that it is locked into position.

② Close the lid, select the DOUGH setting and press START.

③ Add the dried fruit at the buzzer or after the first kneading.

④ When the cycle is complete, carefully remove the pan and tip the dough out on to a lightly floured work surface.

⑤ Knock back the dough and divide into 8–10 equal-sized pieces. Shape into smooth balls and cut a cross on the top of each with a sharp knife.

⑥ Place on a lightly greased baking (cookie) sheet. Cover with lightly greased clingfilm (plastic wrap) and leave in a warm place to prove for about 20 minutes.

⑦ To make the glaze, mix together the egg and water and brush all over the surface of the buns.

⑧ Bake in a preheated oven at 190ºC/375ºF/gas mark 5 (fan oven 170ºC) for about 15 minutes.

DOUGH SETTING
PLUS 45 MINUTES SHAPING, RISING AND BAKING

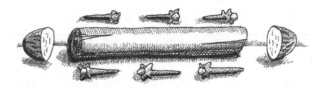

Cracked wheat granary clovers
MAKES 8

For the dough:
275 ml/9 fl oz/generous 1 cup water
30 ml/2 tbsp dried milk powder (non-fat dry milk)
20 ml/1½ tbsp caster (superfine) sugar
5 ml/1 tsp salt
40 ml/2½ tbsp sunflower oil
175 g/6 oz/1½ cups strong white bread flour
175 g/6 oz/1½ cups granary flour
6 ml/1¼ tsp traditional active dried yeast
For the topping:
A little milk, for brushing
50 g/2 oz/½ cup cracked wheat

① To make the dough, place all the ingredients in the bread pan in the order listed. Place the pan in the breadmaker, ensuring that it is locked into position.

② Close the lid, select the DOUGH setting and press START.

③ When the cycle is complete, carefully remove the pan and tip the dough out on to a lightly floured work surface.

④ Knock back the dough, then divide into eight equal-sized pieces. Divide each into three small portions and roll each into a smooth ball.

⑤ Place the three balls close together on a lightly greased baking (cookie) sheet to resemble a clover leaf. Repeat with the remaining balls.

⑥ Brush the top of each clover with a little milk, then sprinkle with the cracked wheat.

⑦ Cover loosely with lightly greased clingfilm (plastic wrap) and leave in a warm place to prove for about 20 minutes.

⑧ Bake in a preheated oven at 200°C/400°F/gas mark 6 (fan oven 180°C) for about 10–15 minutes.

DOUGH SETTING
PLUS 45 MINUTES SHAPING, RISING AND BAKING

Sweet breads and teatime favourites

*T*his chapter offers a wide range of ideas for sweet breads to suit all tastes. There are some delicious breads using chocolate and fruits, as well as some traditional old favourites such as teacakes and lardy bread.

Strawberry and apple slice

MAKES 1 MEDIUM LOAF

Eat warm with ice cream, custard or cream.

For the dough:
275 ml/9 fl oz/generous 1 cup water
20 ml/1½ tbsp sunflower oil
1 egg
30 ml/2 tbsp dried milk powder (non-fat dry milk)
5 ml/1 tsp salt
45 ml/3 tbsp sugar
350 g/12 oz/3 cups spelt flour
7.5 ml/1½ tsp traditional active dried yeast
For the filling:
60 ml/4 tbsp strawberry jam (conserve)
2 small cooking (tart) apples, peeled, cored and sliced
A little milk, for brushing

① To make the dough, place all the ingredients in the bread pan in the order listed. Place the pan in the breadmaker, ensuring that it is locked into position.

② Close the lid, select the DOUGH setting and press START.

③ When the cycle is complete, carefully remove the pan and tip the dough out on to a lightly floured work surface.

④ Knock back the dough, then roll out to a 35 cm/14 in square. Cut the square in half and place one half on a lightly greased baking (cookie) sheet.

⑤ Spread this with the jam, leaving a small border all round the outside.

⑥ Scatter the apple slices over the jam and brush round the uncovered edges of the dough with a little water.

⑦ Using a sharp knife, make slits across the other dough square, not right to the edges. Place directly on top of the apple slices and press round the edges to seal.

⑧ Brush the surface with milk, then cover loosely with lightly greased clingfilm (plastic wrap) and leave in a warm place to prove for about 20 minutes.

⑨ Bake in a preheated oven at 220°C/425°F/gas mark 7 (fan oven 200°C) for about 10–15 minutes.

⑩ Transfer to a cooling rack and allow to cool before slicing.

DOUGH SETTING
PLUS 45 MINUTES SHAPING, RISING AND BAKING

Chocolate and raisin bread
MAKES 1 MEDIUM LOAF

Lovely with a cup of tea or coffee.

275 ml/9 fl oz/generous 1 cup water
20 ml/1½ tbsp sunflower oil
75 ml/5 tbsp chocolate spread
45 ml/3 tbsp dried milk powder (non-fat dry milk)
5 ml/1 tsp salt
90 ml/6 tbsp sugar
350 g/12 oz/3 cups strong white bread flour
20 ml/1½ tbsp cocoa (unsweetened chocolate) powder
7.5 ml/1½ tsp traditional active dried yeast
100 g/4 oz/⅔ cup raisins

① Place all the ingredients except the raisins in the bread pan in the order listed. Place the pan in the breadmaker, ensuring that it is locked into position.

② Close the lid, select the BASIC setting and press START.

③ Add the raisins at the buzzer or after the first kneading.

④ When the cycle is complete, carefully remove the pan using oven gloves.

⑤ Tip the loaf out on to a cooling rack and allow to cool before slicing.

BASIC SETTING

Lardy cake

MAKES 1 MEDIUM CAKE

A traditional yeast cake, best eaten warm and buttered.

For the dough:
150 ml/¼ pt/⅔ cup warm milk
1 egg
25 g/1 oz/2 tbsp butter
30 ml/2 tbsp caster (superfine) sugar
7.5 ml/1½ tsp salt
350 g/12 oz/3 cups strong white bread flour
7.5 ml/1½ tsp traditional active dried yeast
For the filling:
100 g/4 oz/½ cup lard (shortening)
100 g/4 oz/½ cup brown sugar, plus extra for topping
50 g/2 oz/⅓ cup dried mixed fruit (fruit cake mix)

① To make the dough, place all the ingredients in the bread pan in the order listed. Place the pan in the breadmaker, ensuring that it is locked into position.

② Close the lid, select the DOUGH setting and press START.

③ Meanwhile, to make the filling, combine the lard and sugar and divide into five equal-sized pieces.

④ When the cycle is complete, carefully remove the pan and tip the dough out on to a lightly floured work surface.

⑤ Knock back the dough, then roll out to a rectangle about the size of a sheet of A4 paper.

⑥ Spread the dough with a portion of the lard and sugar mixture and sprinkle with a little of the dried fruit. Fold the top third of the dough down and the bottom third up, flaky pastry(paste)-style, then push down around the edges with a rolling pin to seal.

⑦ Give the dough a quarter turn, then repeat the process.

⑧ Repeat three more times until the lard, sugar and dried fruit are used up.

⑨ Fold into three as before and flatten the dough slightly. Mark the top with a few criss-cross cuts and sprinkle with a little brown sugar.

⑩ Place on a lightly greased baking (cookie) sheet. Cover with lightly greased clingfilm (plastic wrap) and leave in a warm place to prove for about 20 minutes.

⑪ Bake in a preheated oven at 200°C/400°F/gas mark 6 (fan oven 180°C) for about 30–45 minutes to ensure the base is thoroughly cooked.

DOUGH SETTING
PLUS 1–1¾ HOURS SHAPING, RISING AND BAKING

Double chocolate and hazelnut bread

MAKES 1 MEDIUM LOAF

275 ml/9 fl oz/generous 1 cup water
20 ml/1½ tbsp sunflower oil
90 ml/6 tbsp chocolate and hazelnut (filbert) spread
30 ml/2 tbsp dried milk powder (non-fat dry milk)
5 ml/1 tsp salt
30 ml/2 tbsp sugar
350 g/12 oz/3 cups strong white bread flour
7.5 ml/1½ tsp traditional active dried yeast
75 g/3 oz/¾ cup plain (semi-sweet) chocolate, broken into
   squares
100 g/4 oz/1 cup hazelnuts

① Place all the ingredients except the chocolate and nuts in the bread pan in the order listed. Place the pan in the breadmaker, ensuring that it is locked into position.

② Close the lid, select the BASIC setting and press START.

③ Add the chocolate and nuts at the buzzer or after the first kneading.

④ When the cycle is complete, carefully remove the pan using oven gloves.

⑤ Tip the loaf out on to a cooling rack and allow to cool before slicing.

BASIC SETTING

Cornish clotted cream heavies

MAKES 8

These rich buns have a close, scone(biscuit)-like texture due to the amount of fat in the recipe. They are delicious eaten warm from the oven with butter, or cooled then split and toasted.

2.5 ml/½ tsp saffron strands
30 ml/2 tbsp milk
100 g/4 oz/½ cup clotted cream, warmed
30 ml/2 tbsp butter
1 egg
2.5 ml/½ tsp salt
50 g/2 oz/¼ cup sugar
2.5 ml/½ tsp ground cinnamon
350 g/12 oz/3 cups strong white bread flour
10 ml/2 tsp traditional active dried yeast
75 g/3 oz/½ cup dried mixed fruit (fruit cake mix)

1. Place all the ingredients except the dried fruit in the bread pan in the order listed. Place the pan in the breadmaker, ensuring that it is locked into position.

2. Close the lid, select the DOUGH setting and press START.

3. Add the dried fruit at the buzzer or after the first kneading.

4. When the cycle is complete, carefully remove the pan and tip the dough out on to a lightly floured work surface.

5. Knock back the dough and divide into eight equal-sized pieces. Roll each into a smooth ball, then flatten very slightly.

6. Place on a lightly greased baking (cookie) sheet, cover with lightly greased clingfilm (plastic wrap) and leave in a warm place to prove for about 30 minutes.

7. Bake in a preheated oven at 200°C/400°F/gas mark 6 (fan oven 180°C) for about 15 minutes.

DOUGH SETTING
PLUS 50 MINUTES SHAPING, RISING AND BAKING

fast orange and cardamom bread

MAKES 1 MEDIUM LOAF

This bread is made using the RAPID setting that many breadmakers have. It is important to use fast-acting yeast and warm (30–35°C/85–95°F) water for the bread to be successful.

---

15 ml/1 tbsp cardamom pods
Juice of 2 oranges
25 g/1 oz/2 tbsp butter, softened
Grated zest of 2 oranges
5 ml/1 tsp salt
60 ml/4 tbsp sugar
350 g/12 oz/3 cups strong white bread flour
7.5 ml/1½ tsp fast-acting yeast

---

① Crush the cardamom pods and discard the husks.

② Make up the orange juice to 275 ml/9 fl oz/generous 1 cup with warm water.

③ Place the cardamom seeds and orange liquid in the bread pan and add the remaining ingredients in the order listed. Place the pan in the breadmaker, ensuring that it is locked into position.

④ Close the lid, select the RAPID setting and press START.

⑤ When the cycle is complete, carefully remove the pan using oven gloves.

⑥ Tip the loaf out on to a cooling rack and allow to cool before slicing.

RAPID SETTING

Toffee bread

MAKES 1 MEDIUM LOAF

A very naughty but nice bread for adults and kids alike!

150 ml/¼ pt/⅔ cup warm milk
1 egg
25 g/1 oz/2 tbsp butter
30 ml/2 tbsp caster (superfine) sugar
7.5 ml/1½ tsp salt
350 g/12 oz/3 cups strong white bread flour
7.5 ml/1½ tsp fast-acting yeast
8 hard toffees, broken into small pieces
75 ml/5 tbsp toffee fudge spread

① Place all the ingredients except the toffees and toffee spread in the bread pan in the order listed. Place the pan in the breadmaker, ensuring that it is locked into position.

② Close the lid, select the DOUGH setting and press START.

③ When the cycle is complete, carefully remove the pan and tip the dough out on to a lightly floured work surface.

④ Knock back the dough, then knead in the toffee pieces.

⑤ Roll out to a little larger than a sheet of A4 paper, then spread with the toffee spread. Fold in half and seal the edges.

⑥ Place on a lightly greased baking (cookie) sheet, cover with lightly greased clingfilm (plastic wrap) and leave in a warm place to prove for about 20 minutes.

⑦ Bake in a preheated oven at 200°C/400°F/gas mark 6 (fan oven 180°C) for about 15 minutes.

DOUGH SETTING
PLUS 40 MINUTES SHAPING, RISING AND BAKING

Peach crescent

MAKES 1 MEDIUM LOAF

This is a very fruity bread that is good as a dessert. Ring the changes by using other dried fruits in place of the peaches.

For the dough:
150 ml/¼ pt/⅔ cup warm milk
1 egg
30 ml/2 tbsp butter
30 ml/2 tbsp caster (superfine) sugar
7.5 ml/1½ tsp salt
350 g/12 oz/3 cups strong white bread flour
7.5 ml/1½ tsp traditional active dried yeast
For the filling:
250 g/9 oz packet of sweetened dried peaches, chopped
50 g/2 oz/¼ cup butter, softened
50 g/2 oz/¼ cup soft brown sugar

① To make the dough, place all the ingredients in the bread pan in the order listed. Place the pan in the breadmaker, ensuring that it is locked into position.

② Close the lid, select the DOUGH setting and press START. When the cycle is complete, carefully remove the pan and tip the dough out on to a lightly floured work surface.

③ Knock back the dough, then roll out to a little larger than a sheet of A4 paper.

④ Scatter the chopped peaches over the dough, then dot with the butter. Sprinkle the sugar over.

⑤ Roll up, Swiss (jelly) roll-style, bend round to form a crescent and place on a lightly greased baking (cookie) sheet with the join underneath. Cover with lightly greased clingfilm (plastic wrap) and leave in a warm place to prove for about 20 minutes.

⑥ Bake in a preheated oven at 200°C/400°F/gas mark 6 (fan oven 180°C) for about 15 minutes.

DOUGH SETTING
PLUS 45 MINUTES SHAPING, RISING AND BAKING

fast vanilla bread

MAKES 1 MEDIUM LOAF

This bread is made using the RAPID cycle that many breadmakers have. It is important to use fast-acting yeast and warm (30–35º/85–95ºF) liquid for the bread to be successful.

275 ml/9 fl oz/generous 1 cup warm milk
1 seed from a vanilla pod
30 ml/2 tbsp butter, softened
5 ml/1 tsp salt
90 ml/6 tbsp sugar
350 g/12 oz/3 cups strong white bread flour
10 ml/2 tsp fast-acting yeast

① Warm the milk with the vanilla seed until just simmering, then remove from the heat and allow to cool until it reaches blood temperature.

② Pour into the bread pan with the vanilla seed, then add all the remaining ingredients in the order listed. Place the pan in the breadmaker, ensuring that it is locked into position.

③ Close the lid, select the RAPID setting and press START.

④ When the cycle is complete, carefully remove the pan using oven gloves.

⑤ Tip the loaf out on to a cooling rack and allow to cool before slicing.

RAPID SETTING

Almond twists

MAKES ABOUT 20

A great snack to go with coffee.

For the dough:
150 ml/¼ pt/⅔ cup warm milk
1 egg
30 ml/2 tbsp butter
30 ml/2 tbsp caster (superfine) sugar
7.5 ml/1½ tsp salt
350 g/12 oz/3 cups strong white bread flour
7.5 ml/1½ tsp traditional active dried yeast
For the filling:
100 g/4 oz/1 cup ground almonds
75 g/3 oz/½ cup icing (confectioners') sugar
100 g/4 oz/½ cup butter, softened
For the glaze and topping:
1 egg, beaten
10 ml/2 tsp water
50 g/2 oz/½ cup flaked (slivered) almonds

① To make the dough, place the all ingredients in the bread pan in the order listed. Place the pan in the breadmaker, ensuring that it is locked into position.

② Close the lid, select the DOUGH setting and press START.

③ When the cycle is complete, carefully remove the pan and tip the dough out on to a lightly floured work surface.

④ Knock back the dough, then roll out to a 30 cm/12 in square.

⑤ To make the filling, combine all the ingredients and spread over one half of the surface of the dough. Fold the other half over the top and press down gently.

⑥ Cut the dough into thin 15 cm/6 in long strips. Twist each strip several times, then transfer to a lightly greased baking (cookie) sheet. Cover with lightly greased clingfilm (plastic wrap) and leave in a warm place to prove for about 20 minutes.

⑦ To make the glaze, mix together the egg and water and beat lightly. Brush all over the surface of the twists, then press the flaked almonds all over.

⑧ Bake in a preheated oven at 220°C/425°F/gas mark 7 (fan oven 200°C) for about 10 minutes.

DOUGH SETTING
PLUS 40 MINUTES SHAPING, RISING AND BAKING

Lemon and lime marmalade bread
MAKES 1 MEDIUM LOAF

A tangy bread, best eaten warm and buttered.

275 ml/9 fl oz/generous 1 cup water
40 ml/2½ tbsp sunflower oil
75 ml/5 tbsp lemon and lime marmalade
30 ml/2 tbsp dried milk powder (non-fat dry milk)
5 ml/1 tsp salt
350 g/12 oz/3 cups strong white bread flour
7.5 ml/1½ tsp traditional active dried yeast

① Place all the ingredients in the bread pan in the order listed. Place the pan in the breadmaker, ensuring that it is locked into position.

② Close the lid, select the BASIC setting and press START.

③ When the cycle is complete, carefully remove the pan using oven gloves.

④ Tip the loaf out on to a cooling rack and allow to cool before slicing.

BASIC SETTING

Teacakes
MAKES 8

Serve these warm from the oven, split and buttered, or allow to cool and toast and butter later.

For the dough:
150 ml/¼ pt/⅔ cup warm milk
1 egg
30 ml/2 tbsp butter
30 ml/2 tbsp caster (superfine) sugar
7.5 ml/1½ tsp salt
350 g/12 oz/3 cups strong white bread flour
7.5 ml/1½ tsp traditional active dried yeast
100 g/4 oz/⅔ cup currants
30 ml/2 tbsp chopped mixed (candied) peel
For the glaze:
1 egg, beaten
10 ml/2 tsp water

① To make the dough, place all the ingredients except the currants and peel in the bread pan in the order listed. Place the pan in the breadmaker, ensuring that it is locked into position.

② Close the lid, select the DOUGH setting and press START.

③ Add the currants and peel at the buzzer or after the first kneading.

④ When the cycle is complete, carefully remove the pan and tip the dough out on to a lightly floured work surface.

⑤ Knock back the dough, then divide into eight equal-sized pieces. Shape into smooth balls, then flatten slightly.

⑥ Place on a lightly greased baking (cookie) sheet, cover with lightly greased clingfilm (plastic wrap) and leave in a warm place to prove for about 20 minutes.

⑦ To make the glaze, mix together the egg and water and brush all over the surface of the teacakes.

⑧ Bake in a preheated oven at 220°C/425°F/gas mark 7 (fan oven 200°C) for about 15 minutes.

DOUGH SETTING
PLUS 40 MINUTES SHAPING, RISING AND BAKING

Double banana bread
MAKES 1 MEDIUM LOAF

Eat warm with butter and honey.

275 ml/9 fl oz/generous 1 cup water
30 ml/2 tbsp sunflower oil
10 ml/2 tsp honey
1 large banana, mashed
30 ml/2 tbsp dried milk powder (non-fat dry milk)
5 ml/1 tsp salt
350 g/12 oz/3 cups strong white bread flour
45 ml/3 tbsp wheatgerm
7.5 ml/1½ tsp traditional active dried yeast
100 g/4 oz/⅔ cup yoghurt-coated dried banana

① Place all the ingredients except the dried banana in the bread pan in the order listed. Place the pan in the breadmaker, ensuring that it is locked into position.

② Close the lid, select the BASIC setting and press START.

③ Add the dried banana at the buzzer or after the first kneading.

④ When the cycle is complete, carefully remove the pan using oven gloves.

⑤ Tip the loaf out on to a cooling rack and allow to cool before slicing.

BASIC SETTING

Devonshire splits
MAKES 8

Spoil yourself with these cream-filled delights! Try ringing the changes by filling with your favourite jam (conserve).

For the dough:
150 ml/¼ pt/⅔ cup warm milk
1 egg
30 ml/2 tbsp butter
30 ml/2 tbsp caster (superfine) sugar
7.5 ml/1½ tsp salt
350 g/12 oz/3 cups strong white bread flour
7.5 ml/1½ tsp traditional active dried yeast
For the glaze:
1 egg, beaten
10 ml/2 tsp water
For the filling:
175 g/6 oz/½ cup strawberry jam
150 ml/¼ pt/⅔ cup double (heavy) or whipping cream,
   whipped

① To make the dough, place all the ingredients in the bread pan in the order listed. Place the pan in the breadmaker, ensuring that it is locked into position.

② Close the lid, select the DOUGH setting and press START.

③ When the cycle is complete, carefully remove the pan and tip the dough out on to a lightly floured work surface.

④ Knock back the dough, then divide into eight equal-sized pieces. Shape into smooth balls, then draw them out slightly into a 'bullet' shape.

⑤ Place on a lightly greased baking (cookie) sheet, cover with lightly greased clingfilm (plastic wrap) and leave in a warm place to prove for about 20 minutes.

⑥ To make the glaze, mix together the egg and water and brush all over the surface of the dough.

⑦ Bake in a preheated oven at 220°C/425°F/gas mark 7 (fan oven 200°C) for about 15 minutes.

⑧ Transfer to a cooling rack and leave until completely cool.

⑨ To fill, make a central split along the length of each, then fill with the strawberry jam and whipped cream.

DOUGH SETTING
PLUS 45 MINUTES SHAPING, RISING AND BAKING

Milk bread
MAKES 1 LARGE LOAF

Use this recipe to make a moist, rich loaf ideal for sumptuous sandwiches. The dough is also used in some other recipes in this chapter, such as teacakes, Devonshire splits and almond twists.

250 ml/8 fl oz/1 cup warm milk
1 egg
50 g/2 oz/¼ cup butter
60 ml/4 tbsp caster (superfine) sugar
10 ml/2 tsp salt
450 g/1 lb/4 cups strong white bread flour
10 ml/2 tsp traditional active dried yeast

① Place all the ingredients in the bread pan in the order listed. Place the pan in the breadmaker, ensuring that it is locked into position.

② Close the lid, select the BASIC setting and press START.

③ When the cycle is complete, carefully remove the pan using oven gloves.

④ Tip the loaf out on to a cooling rack and allow to cool before slicing.

BASIC SETTING

ℱpple and almond puffs
MAKES 8

Eat these warm with cream and a cup of hot coffee.

For the dough:
300 ml/½ pt/1¼ cups water
30 ml/2 tbsp sunflower oil
7.5 ml/1½ tsp salt
10 ml/2 tsp sugar
15 ml/1 tbsp dried milk powder (non-fat dry milk)
450 g/1 lb/4 cups strong white bread flour
7.5 ml/1½ tsp traditional active dried yeast
For the filling:
50 g/2 oz/¼ cup butter, softened
50 g/2 oz/¼ cup soft brown sugar
50 g/2 oz/½ cup ground almonds
2 large eating (dessert) apples, peeled and finely chopped
A little milk, for brushing

① To make the dough, place all the ingredients in the bread pan in the order listed. Place the pan in the breadmaker, ensuring that it is locked into position.

② Close the lid, select the DOUGH setting and press START.

③ Meanwhile, to make the filling, cream together the butter, sugar and almonds.

④ When the cycle is complete, carefully remove the pan and tip the dough out on to a lightly floured work surface.

⑤ Knock back the dough, then divide into 16 equal-sized pieces. Roll each out to a 13 cm/5 in diameter round.

⑥ Divide the almond mixture between eight of the rounds, spreading it in the centre and leaving a 1 cm/½ in margin all round. Top with the chopped apple.

⑦ Brush around the borders with a little water, then cut about three slits in the centre of the remaining eight rounds. Place them over the apple filling and pinch well around the edges to seal. Brush all over with milk.

⑧ Place on a lightly greased baking (cookie) sheet. Cover loosely with clingfilm (plastic wrap) and leave in a warm place to prove for about 30 minutes.

⑨ Bake in a preheated oven at 200°C/400°F/gas mark 6 (fan oven 180°C) for about 20 minutes until golden and puffy. Serve while still warm.

DOUGH SETTING
PLUS 1 HOUR SHAPING, RISING AND BAKING

Apple muffins
MAKES 16

Eat warm and buttered with an extra sprinkling of brown sugar as a teatime treat.

30 ml/2 tbsp water
75 ml/5 tbsp milk
1 egg
15 ml/1 tbsp sunflower oil
45 ml/3 tbsp sugar
2.5 ml/½ tsp salt
1 cooking (tart) apple, peeled, cored and finely chopped
2.5 ml/½ tsp ground cinnamon
100 g/4 oz/1 cup strong white bread flour
100 g/4 oz/1 cup spelt flour
7.5 ml/1½ tsp traditional active dried yeast

① Place all the ingredients in the bread pan in the order listed. Place the pan in the breadmaker, ensuring that it is locked into position.

② Close the lid, select the DOUGH setting and press START.

③ When the cycle is complete, carefully remove the pan and tip the dough out on to a lightly floured work surface.

④ Knock back the dough and divide into 16 equal-sized pieces. Roll each into a smooth ball, then flatten to about 1 cm/½ in thick.

⑤ Place on a lightly greased baking (cookie) sheet, cover with lightly greased clingfilm (plastic wrap) and leave in a warm place to prove for about 10 minutes.

⑥ Bake in a preheated oven at 230°C/450°F/gas mark 8 (fan oven 210°C) for about 5 minutes, then turn them over and cook for a further 5 minutes. Eat warm.

DOUGH SETTING
PLUS 25 MINUTES SHAPING, RISING AND BAKING

Mixed fruit, orange and syrup bread
MAKES 1 LARGE LOAF

Simply butter and enjoy with a cup of Earl Grey tea.

Juice of 4 oranges
60 ml/4 tbsp sunflower oil
60 ml/4 tbsp golden (light corn) syrup
5 ml/1 tsp salt
60 ml/4 tbsp dried milk powder (non-fat dry milk)
Finely grated zest of 4 oranges
450 g/1 lb/4 cups strong white bread flour
10 ml/2 tsp traditional active dried yeast
100 g/4 oz/⅔ cup dried mixed fruit (fruit cake mix)

① Place all the ingredients except the dried fruit in the bread pan in the order listed. Place the pan in the breadmaker, ensuring that it is locked into position.

② Close the lid, select the BASIC setting and press START.

③ Add the dried fruit at the buzzer or after the first kneading.

④ When the cycle is complete, carefully remove the pan using oven gloves.

⑤ Tip the loaf out on to a cooling rack and allow to cool before slicing.

BASIC SETTING

Apricot and cinnamon ring
MAKES 1 LARGE LOAF

This bread is equally good as a dessert or as a teatime treat.

For the dough:
250 ml/8 fl oz/1 cup water
2 eggs
45 ml/3 tbsp dried milk powder (non-fat dry milk)
5 ml/1 tsp salt
90 ml/6 tbsp sugar
10 ml/2 tsp ground cinnamon
50 g/2 oz/¼ cup butter
400 g/14 oz/3½ cups strong white bread flour
7.5 ml/1½ tsp traditional active dried yeast
225 g/8 oz/1⅓ cups no-need-to-soak dried apricots
For the filling:
100 g/4 oz/½ cup butter, softened
100 g/4 oz/½ cup sugar
5 ml/1 tsp ground cinnamon
Melted butter, for brushing
For the icing (frosting):
90 ml/6 tbsp icing (confectioners') sugar
20 ml/4 tsp water
A few drops of vanilla essence (extract)

① To make the dough, place all the ingredients except the apricots in the bread pan in the order listed. Place the pan in the breadmaker, ensuring that it is locked into position.

② Close the lid, select the DOUGH setting and press START.

③ Add the apricots at the buzzer or after the first kneading.

④ Meanwhile, to make the filling, combine the butter, sugar and cinnamon.

⑤ When the cycle is complete, carefully remove the pan and tip the dough out on to a lightly floured work surface.

⑥ Knock back the dough and roll out to a 30 × 45 cm/ 12 × 18 in rectangle. Spread all over with the butter mixture.

⑦ Roll up along the long edge, then form into a round and pinch the two dough ends together. Use scissors to make cuts at intervals all the way round the dough roll at 45° angles.

⑧ Pull each section out slightly and twist to a horizontal position. Brush all over with melted butter, then cover loosely with clingfilm (plastic wrap) and leave in a warm place to prove for about 20 minutes.

⑨ Bake in a preheated oven at 190°C/375°F/gas mark 5 (fan oven 170°C) for 20–25 minutes.

⑩ Meanwhile, combine the icing ingredients.

⑪ Remove the ring from the oven and place on a cooling rack. Drizzle the icing over while still warm.

DOUGH SETTING
PLUS 1 HOUR SHAPING, RISING AND BAKING

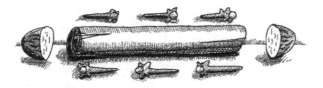

Double chocolate doughnuts
MAKES 10–12

For the dough:
275 ml/9 fl oz/generous 1 cup water
50 g/2 oz/½ cup cocoa (unsweetened chocolate) powder
30 ml/2 tbsp dried milk powder (non-fat dry milk)
30 ml/2 tbsp caster (superfine) sugar, plus extra for
  coating
5 ml/1 tsp salt
40 ml/2½ tbsp sunflower oil
350 g/12 oz/3 cups strong white bread flour
6 ml/1¼ tsp traditional active dried yeast
For the filling:
125 g/4½ oz/1 small bar of milk (sweet) chocolate,
  separated into 10–12 squares
Oil, for deep-frying
15 ml/1 tbsp cocoa powder

① To make the dough, warm the water and stir in the cocoa powder until dissolved. Cool to lukewarm.

② Pour into the bread pan, then add the remaining ingredients in the order listed. Place the pan in the breadmaker, ensuring that it is locked into position.

③ Close the lid, select the DOUGH setting and press START.

④ When the cycle is complete, carefully remove the pan and turn the dough out on to a lightly floured work surface.

⑤ Knock back the dough, then divide into 10–12 equal-sized pieces. Roll each into a ball, then flatten slightly.

⑥ Place a piece of chocolate in the middle of each. Carefully pinch the edges up around the chocolate and form back into balls.

⑦ Place on a plate or a baking (cookie) sheet. Cover with lightly greased clingfilm (plastic wrap) and leave in a warm place to prove for about 20 minutes.

⑧ Heat the oil in a large saucepan or deep fat fryer to just below smoking point.

⑨ Carefully deep-fry a few doughnuts at a time until golden brown, then drain on kitchen paper (paper towels).

⑩ Combine the cocoa with the extra caster sugar and roll the doughnuts in the mixture while still hot.

DOUGH SETTING
PLUS 45 MINUTES SHAPING, RISING AND COOKING

Coffee and brazil nut bread
MAKES 1 LARGE LOAF

This bread is best eaten warm with strong, hot coffee.

250 ml/8 fl oz/1 cup water
45 ml/3 tbsp coffee essence (extract)
15 ml/1 tbsp caster (superfine) sugar
45 ml/3 tbsp dried milk powder (non-fat dry milk)
7.5 ml/1½ tsp salt
30 ml/2 tbsp sunflower oil
225 g/8 oz/2 cups strong white bread flour
225 g/8 oz/2 cups strong wholemeal bread flour
7.5 ml/1½ tsp traditional active dried yeast
75 g/3 oz/¾ cup brazil nuts, coarsely chopped

① Place all the ingredients except the nuts in the bread pan in the order listed. Place the pan in the breadmaker, ensuring that it is locked into position.

② Close the lid, select the BASIC setting and press START.

③ Add the nuts at the buzzer or after the first kneading.

④ When the cycle is complete, carefully remove the pan using oven gloves.

⑤ Tip the loaf out on to a cooling rack and allow to cool before slicing.

BASIC SETTING

Cherry flip-overs
MAKES 10–12

Eat hot for dessert with plenty of whipped cream!

For the dough:
275 ml/9 fl oz/generous 1 cup water
30 ml/2 tbsp dried milk powder (non-fat dry milk)
20 ml/1½ tbsp caster (superfine) sugar, plus extra for
  coating
5 ml/1 tsp salt
40 ml/2½ tbsp sunflower oil
350 g/12 oz/3 cups strong white bread flour
6 ml/1¼ tsp traditional active dried yeast
For the filling:
400 g/14 oz/1 large can of cherry pie filling
Oil, for deep-frying

① To make the dough, place all the ingredients in the bread pan in the order listed. Place the pan in the breadmaker, ensuring that it is locked into position.

② Close the lid, select the DOUGH setting and press START.

③ When the cycle is complete, carefully remove the pan and turn the dough out on to a lightly floured work surface.

④ Knock back the dough, then divide into 10–12 equal-sized pieces and roll into balls. Press out each ball to a flat oval.

⑤ Place a spoonful of the pie filling in the centre of each oval, damp the edges with water, then fold each oval in half and pinch the edges together to seal.

⑥ Place on a plate or a baking (cookie) sheet. Cover with lightly greased clingfilm (plastic wrap) and leave in a warm place to prove for about 10 minutes.

⑦ Heat the oil in a large saucepan or deep fat fryer to just below smoking point.

⑧ Carefully deep-fry a few flip-overs at a time until golden brown, then drain on kitchen paper (paper towels). Roll in caster sugar while still hot.

DOUGH SETTING
PLUS 45 MINUTES SHAPING, RISING AND COOKING

Apricot and cream cheese loaf
MAKES 1 LARGE LOAF

A treat spread with butter or extra cream cheese.

---

275 ml/9 fl oz/generous 1 cup water
40 ml/2½ tbsp sunflower oil
100 g/4 oz/½ cup cream cheese
30 ml/2 tbsp dried milk powder (non-fat dry milk)
20 ml/1½ tbsp caster (superfine) sugar
5 ml/1 tsp salt
225 g/8 oz/2 cups strong white bread flour
175 g/6 oz/1½ cups strong wholemeal bread flour
6 ml/1¼ tsp traditional active dried yeast
50 g/2 oz/½ cup almonds, chopped
100 g/4 oz/⅔ cup no-need-to-soak dried apricots, halved

---

① Place all the ingredients except the almonds and apricots in the bread pan in the order listed. Place the pan in the breadmaker, ensuring that it is locked into position.

② Close the lid, select the WHOLEMEAL setting and press START.

③ Add the almonds and apricots at the buzzer or after the first kneading.

④ When the cycle is complete, carefully remove the pan using oven gloves.

⑤ Tip the loaf out on to a cooling rack and allow to cool before slicing.

WHOLEMEAL SETTING

Sweet potato, honey and peanut loaf

MAKES 1 MEDIUM LOAF

Try this bread alongside a mild curry or simply with grilled (broiled) smoked bacon.

175 ml/6 fl oz/¾ cup water
175 g/6 oz mashed cooked sweet potato
60 ml/4 tbsp olive oil
60 ml/4 tbsp honey
45 ml/3 tbsp dried milk powder (non-fat dry milk)
7.5 ml/1½ tsp salt
20 ml/4 tsp English mustard powder
50 g/2 oz/½ cup dry roasted peanuts
225 g/8 oz/2 cups strong white bread flour
100 g/4 oz/1 cup strong wholemeal bread flour
7.5 ml/1½ tsp traditional active dried yeast

① Place all the ingredients in the bread pan in the order listed. Place the pan in the breadmaker, ensuring that it is locked into position.

② Close the lid, select the WHOLEMEAL setting and press START.

③ When the cycle is complete, carefully remove the pan using oven gloves.

④ Tip the loaf out on to a cooling rack and allow to cool before slicing.

WHOLEMEAL SETTING

fig and brandy bread
MAKES 1 MEDIUM LOAF

This is a rich, boozy bread, that would make a good addition to the Christmas fare.

---

60 ml/4 tbsp brandy
175 g/6 oz/1 cup dried figs, roughly chopped
175 ml/6 fl oz/¾ cup milk
50 g/2 oz/¼ cup butter, softened
1 egg
5 ml/1 tsp salt
60 ml/4 tbsp soft brown sugar
350 g/12 oz/3 cups strong white bread flour
7.5 ml/1½ tsp traditional active dried yeast

---

① Warm the brandy, then pour it over the figs. Leave to soak for 30 minutes.

② Drain the brandy from the figs and pour into the bread pan. Add all the remaining ingredients except the figs in the order listed. Place the pan in the breadmaker, ensuring that it is locked into position.

③ Close the lid, select the BASIC setting and press START.

④ Add the figs when the buzzer sounds or after the first kneading.

⑤ When the cycle is complete, carefully remove the pan using oven gloves.

⑥ Tip the loaf out on to a cooling rack and allow to cool before slicing.

BASIC SETTING

Earl Grey raisin loaf
MAKES 1 LARGE LOAF

Simply butter and enjoy by the fireside.

375 ml/13 fl oz/1½ cups boiling water
2 Earl Grey tea bags
175 g/6 oz/1 cup raisins
60 ml/4 tbsp dried milk powder (non-fat dry milk)
60 ml/4 tbsp caster (superfine) sugar
5 ml/1 tsp salt
60 ml/4 tbsp sunflower oil
450 g/1 lb/4 cups strong white bread flour
10 ml/2 tsp traditional active dried yeast

① Make a pot of tea by pouring the boiling water over the tea bags. Pour over the raisins and leave for 1–2 hours.

② Drain the tea from the raisins and pour into the bread pan. Add the remaining ingredients except the raisins in the order listed. Place the pan in the breadmaker, ensuring that it is locked into position.

③ Close the lid, select the BASIC setting and press START.

④ Add the raisins at the buzzer or after the first kneading.

⑤ When the cycle is complete, carefully remove the pan using oven gloves.

⑥ Tip the loaf out on to a cooling rack and allow to cool before slicing.

BASIC SETTING

Double chocolate and orange bread

MAKES 1 LARGE LOAF

Sheer indulgence! Best served warm with butter or whipped cream and a cup of hot chocolate on the side.

30 ml/2 tbsp cocoa (unsweetened chocolate) powder
Juice of 1 orange
1 egg
30 ml/2 tbsp dried milk powder (non-fat dry milk)
25 g/1 oz/2 tbsp butter
Grated zest of 1 orange
5 ml/1 tsp salt
60 ml/4 tbsp sugar
100 g/4 oz/1 cup orange-flavoured plain (semi-sweet)
   chocolate, finely chopped
250 g/9 oz/2¼ cups strong white bread flour
250 g/9 oz/2¼ cups strong wholemeal bread flour
5 ml/1 tsp traditional active dried yeast

① Blend the cocoa powder with a little hot water in a measuring jug, then add the orange juice and make up to 300 ml/½ pt/1¼ cups with cold water. Pour into the bread pan.

② Add all the remaining ingredients in the order listed. Place the pan in the breadmaker, ensuring that it is locked into position.

③ Close the lid, select the WHOLEMEAL setting and press START.

④ When the cycle is complete, carefully remove the pan using oven gloves.

⑤ Tip the loaf out on to a cooling rack. Serve warm.

WHOLEMEAL SETTING

Pecan and rose water plait
MAKES 1 LARGE LOAF

This makes a large plaited loaf, good for tearing off in lumps and eating with strong fresh coffee.

For the dough:
250 ml/8 fl oz/1 cup water
60 ml/4 tbsp rose water
1 egg, beaten
90 ml/6 tbsp butter, softened
5 ml/1 tsp salt
25 g/1 oz/2 tbsp sugar
45 ml/3 tbsp milk
450 g/1 lb/4 cups strong white bread flour
7.5 ml/1½ tsp traditional active dried yeast
75 g/3 oz/¾ cup pecan nuts
For the icing (frosting) and topping:
60 ml/4 tbsp rose water
100 g/4 oz/⅔ cup icing (confectioners') sugar
25 g/1 oz/¼ cup pecan nuts, roughly chopped

① To make the dough, place all the ingredients except the nuts in the bread pan in the order listed. Place the pan in the breadmaker, ensuring that it is locked into position.

② Close the lid, select the DOUGH setting and press START.

③ Add the pecans when the buzzer sounds or after the first kneading.

④ When the cycle is complete, carefully tip the dough out on to a lightly floured work surface.

⑤ Knock back the dough, then divide into three equal-sized pieces. Roll each into a sausage about 30 cm/12 in long.

⑥ Pinch all three together at one end and plait, tucking the ends under slightly.

⑦ Place on a lightly greased baking (cookie) sheet. Cover loosely with clingfilm (plastic wrap) and leave in a warm place to prove for 20 minutes.

⑧ Bake at 200°C/400°F/gas mark 6 (fan oven 180°C) for about 20 minutes until golden.

⑨ Meanwhile, make the icing by combining the rose water and icing sugar.

⑩ Place the loaf on a cooling rack and, while still warm, drizzle the icing over and scatter with the chopped nuts.

DOUGH SETTING
PLUS 50 MINUTES SHAPING, RISING AND BAKING

Rich breakfast honey bread
MAKES 1 LARGE LOAF

This bread is ideal for breakfast, either sliced and buttered or served with grilled (broiled) bacon.

250 ml/8 fl oz/1 cup warm water
30 ml/2 tbsp honey
1 egg
50 g/2 oz/¼ cup butter
7.5 ml/1½ tsp salt
30 ml/2 tbsp sugar
60 ml/4 tbsp dried milk powder (non-fat dry milk)
450 g/1 lb/4 cups strong white bread flour
5 ml/1 tsp traditional active dried yeast

① Place all the ingredients in the bread pan in the order listed. Place the pan in the breadmaker, ensuring that it is locked into position.

② Close the lid, select the BASIC setting and press START.

③ When the cycle is complete, carefully remove the pan using oven gloves.

④ Tip the loaf out on to a cooling rack and allow to cool before slicing.

BASIC SETTING

Pear streusel küchen

MAKES 1 MEDIUM CAKE

More like a cake or tart than a bread, this German-style dish is a coffee-time treat!

For the dough:
150 ml/¼ pt/⅔ cup warm milk
1 egg
30 ml/2 tbsp butter
30 ml/2 tbsp caster (superfine) sugar
2.5 ml/½ tsp salt
350 g/12 oz/3 cups strong white bread flour
5 ml/1 tsp ground cinnamon
7.5 ml/1½ tsp traditional active dried yeast
For the topping:
450 g/1 lb/1 very large can of pear slices or quarters, drained
50 g/2 oz/½ cup plain (all-purpose) flour
25 g/1 oz/2 tbsp sugar
50 g/2 oz/¼ cup butter, softened
A little milk, for brushing

① To make the dough, place all the ingredients in the bread pan in the order listed. Place the pan in the breadmaker, ensuring that it is locked into position.

② Close the lid, select the DOUGH setting and press START.

③ When the cycle is complete, carefully remove the pan and tip the dough out on to a lightly floured work surface.

④ Knock back the dough and roll out to line a greased baking (cookie) sheet about 30 × 20 cm/12 × 8 in.

⑤ To make the topping, arrange the pear slices attractively all over the dough.

⑥ Combine the flour and sugar, then rub in the butter. Sprinkle all over the pears.

⑦ Brush the edges of the dough with milk.

⑧ Cover with lightly greased clingfilm (plastic) wrap and leave in a warm place to prove for about 20 minutes.

⑨ Bake in a preheated oven at 200°C/400°F/gas mark 6 (fan oven 180°C) for about 20 minutes.

DOUGH SETTING
PLUS 1 HOUR SHAPING, RISING AND BAKING

Maraschino cherry and nut loaf
MAKES 1 LARGE LOAF

A lovely moist tea bread that needs nothing more than a little butter.

---

120 ml/4 fl oz/½ cup maraschino cherry syrup
250 ml/8 fl oz/1 cup water
15 ml/1 tbsp dried milk powder (non-fat dry milk)
5 ml/1 tsp salt
60 ml/4 tbsp butter
175 g/6 oz/¾ cup maraschino cherries
75 g/3 oz/¾ cup mixed nuts such as walnuts, hazelnuts (filberts), brazil nuts, almonds, roughly chopped
450 g/1 lb/4 cups strong white bread flour
7.5 ml/1½ tsp traditional active dried yeast

---

① Place all the ingredients in the bread pan in the order listed. Place the pan in the breadmaker, ensuring that it is locked into position.

② Close the lid, select the BASIC setting and press START.

③ When the cycle is complete, carefully remove the pan using oven gloves.

④ Tip the loaf out on to a cooling rack and allow to cool before slicing.

BASIC SETTING

Cakes, jam and odds and ends

*T*his final chapter explores some of the functions of the most sophisticated breadmakers, so you'll only be able to try these recipes if your breadmaker has the appropriate cycle programmes.

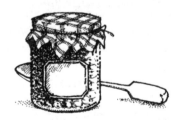

Basic cake mixture
MAKES 1 MEDIUM CAKE

Some of the instruction manuals I have looked at for breadmakers with the CAKE cycle suggest pre-mixing the ingredients in two separate bowls, i.e. butter, eggs and liquids in one bowl and the dry ingredients in another. Personally, I feel this defeats the object of using a machine at all! Consequently, I experimented with adding all the ingredients to the pan without pre-mixing, but liquids first and with the butter or margarine softened. The results I obtained were more than satisfactory and showed no real difference from when I had pre-mixed. However, I recommend you experiment with the different techniques with your breadmaker to see which option gives the best results.

175 g/6 oz/¾ cup butter or margarine, softened
3 eggs
2.5 ml/½ tsp vanilla essence (extract)
15 ml/1 tbsp milk
200 g/7 oz/1¾ cups self-raising (self-rising) flour
100 g/4 oz/½ cup caster (superfine) sugar

① Place all the ingredients in the bread pan in the order listed. Place the pan in the breadmaker, ensuring that it is locked into position.

② Close the lid, select the CAKE setting and press START.

③ When the cycle is complete, turn the machine off and allow the cake to cool in the pan for about 10 minutes.

④ Using oven gloves, carefully remove the pan and transfer the cake to a wire cooling rack. Remove the paddle(s) if still embedded in the base of the cake. Allow to cool completely.

⑤ Either eat the cake as it is, or split it and fill with jam (conserve), whipped cream or butter icing (frosting).

CAKE SETTING

Apple and almond cake
MAKES 1 MEDIUM CAKE

---

175 g/6 oz/¾ cup butter or margarine, softened
2 eggs
175 g/6 oz/1½ cups grated eating (dessert) apple
200 g/7 oz/1¾ cups self-raising (self-rising) flour
100 g/4 oz/½ cup caster (superfine) sugar
75 g/3 oz/¾ cup ground almonds
A pinch of salt
2.5 ml/½ tsp ground cinnamon

---

① Place all the ingredients in the bread pan in the order listed. Place the pan in the breadmaker, ensuring that it is locked into position.

② Close the lid, select the CAKE setting and press START.

③ When the cycle is complete, turn the machine off and allow the cake to cool in the pan for about 10 minutes.

④ Using oven gloves, carefully remove the pan and transfer the cake to a wire cooling rack. Remove the paddle(s) if still embedded in the base of the cake. Allow to cool completely.

⑤ Either eat the cake as it is or split it and fill with jam (conserve), whipped cream or butter icing (frosting).

CAKE SETTING

Mocha cake
MAKES 1 MEDIUM CAKE

10 ml/2 tsp instant coffee powder or granules
7.5 ml/1½ tsp water
175 g/6 oz/¾ cup butter or margarine, softened
3 eggs
15 ml/1 tbsp golden (light corn) syrup
200 g/7 oz/1¾ cups self-raising (self-rising) flour
20 ml/1½ tbsp cocoa (unsweetened chocolate) powder
100 g/4 oz/½ cup caster (superfine) sugar
75 g/3 oz/¾ cup plain (semi-sweet) chocolate, broken
    into small chunks

① Dissolve the coffee in the water, then pour into the bread pan. Add all the remaining ingredients except the chocolate in the order listed. Place the pan in the breadmaker, ensuring that it is locked into position.

② Close the lid, select the CAKE setting and press START.

③ Add the chocolate when the buzzer sounds or after the first kneading.

④ When the cycle is complete, turn the machine off and allow the cake to cool in the pan for about 10 minutes.

⑤ Using oven gloves, carefully remove the pan and transfer the cake to a wire cooling rack. Remove the paddle(s) if still embedded in the base of the cake. Allow to cool completely.

⑥ Either eat the cake as it is or split it and fill with chocolate spread, whipped cream or butter icing (frosting).

CAKE SETTING

Apple and cinnamon jam

MAKES THREE OR FOUR 450 G/1 LB JARS

The time required for this jam (conserve) to reach setting point will depend on the type of apple used and the ripeness of the fruit. Use the EXTRA BAKE cycle to extend the cooking time until setting point has been reached. NEVER open the lid during mixing – jam splashes burn!

This jam is lovely with scones (biscuits) or as a cake filling.

---

700 g/1½ lb apples, peeled, cored and chopped
60 ml/4 tbsp lemon juice
225 g/8 oz/1 cup preserving sugar
7.5 ml/1½ tsp ground cinnamon
30 ml/2 tbsp water

---

① Place all the ingredients in the bread pan in the order listed. Place the pan in the breadmaker, ensuring that it is locked into position.

② Close the lid, select the JAM setting and press START.

③ While the jam is cooking clean and warm the jam jars.

④ Use the EXTRA BAKE cycle to extend the cooking time. Test for a set in the normal way.

⑤ When the setting point is reached, turn the machine off and remove the paddle(s) carefully using a pair of tongs.

⑥ Allow the jam to cool slightly, then use oven gloves to lift out the pan and carefully pour the jam into the warm jars.

⑦ Cover and seal the jars in the normal way.

JAM SETTING

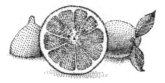

Apple and blackberry jam
MAKES THREE OR FOUR 450 G/1 LB JARS

The time required for this jam (conserve) to reach setting point will depend on the type of apple used and the ripeness of the fruit. Use the EXTRA BAKE cycle to extend the cooking time until setting point has been reached. NEVER open the lid during mixing – jam splashes burn!

This jam is lovely with scones (biscuits) or as a cake filling.

---

450 g/1 lb/4 cups blackberries
225 g/8 oz apples, peeled, cored and chopped
60 ml/4 tbsp lemon juice
225 g/8 oz/1 cup preserving sugar

---

① Place all the ingredients in the bread pan in the order listed. Place the pan in the breadmaker, ensuring that it is locked into position.

② Close the lid, select the JAM setting and press START.

③ While the jam is cooking clean and warm the jam jars.

④ Use the EXTRA BAKE cycle to extend the cooking time. Test for a set in the normal way.

⑤ When the setting point is reached, turn the machine off and remove the paddle(s) carefully using a pair of tongs.

⑥ Allow the jam to cool slightly, then use oven gloves to lift out the pan and carefully pour the jam into the warm jars.

⑦ Cover and seal the jars in the normal way.

JAM SETTING

Rhubarb and ginger jam
MAKES THREE OR FOUR 450 G/1 LB JARS

The time required for this jam (conserve) to reach setting point will depend on the ripeness of the fruit. Use the EXTRA BAKE cycle to extend the cooking time until setting point has been reached. NEVER open the lid during mixing – jam splashes burn!

This jam is delicious on toast or as a filling for tarts and pancakes.

---

450 g/1 lb rhubarb, chopped
60 ml/4 tbsp lemon juice
225 g/8 oz/1 cup preserving sugar
5 ml/1 tsp ground ginger

---

① Place all the ingredients in the bread pan in the order listed. Place the pan in the breadmaker, ensuring that it is locked into position.

② Close the lid, select the JAM setting and press START.

③ While the jam is cooking clean and warm the jam jars.

④ Use the EXTRA BAKE cycle to extend the cooking time. Test for a set in the normal way.

⑤ When the setting point is reached, turn the machine off and remove the paddle(s) carefully using a pair of tongs.

⑥ Allow the jam to cool slightly, then use oven gloves to lift out the pan and carefully pour the jam into the warm jars.

⑦ Cover and seal the jars in the normal way.

JAM SETTING

Pasta

MAKES 175 G/6 OZ PASTA

Some breadmakers now offer a very useful cycle for making pasta dough. If your model does not have this facility, try using the DOUGH cycle but only allow the dough to knead for about 10–15 minutes and then switch off the machine and remove the dough.

This recipe makes a small portion of dough, which I find easier to handle if you are not used to making pasta. Simply double the quantities if you want a larger amount.

3 eggs
175 g/6 oz/1½ cups pasta flour

① Place the ingredients in the bread pan in the order listed. Place the pan in the breadmaker, ensuring that it is locked into position.

② Close the lid, select the PASTA setting and press START.

③ When the cycle is complete, carefully remove the pan and tip the dough out on to a lightly floured work surface.

④ Cover with clingfilm (plastic wrap) and leave to rest for 10 minutes.

PASTA SETTING

To make noodles

① Use either a pasta machine or a rolling pin to roll out the pasta until very thin.

② Cut into thin strips (you choose the thickness you require) and hang over a rack or the back of a chair to dry out.

③ Cook in boiling salted water for about 3–5 minutes depending on the thickness of the noodles.

④ Drain and serve buttered or with your favourite pasta sauce.

Spinach and Brie ravioli

SERVES 4 AS A STARTER OR 2 AS A MAIN COURSE

---

1 quantity of prepared pasta dough (page 153)
100 g/4 oz cold cooked spinach, drained
175 g/6 oz/1½ cups Brie, cubed
1.25 ml/¼ tsp grated nutmeg
A squeeze of lemon juice
Salt and freshly ground black pepper

---

① Roll out the dough to give two rectangular sheets about the size of a sheet of A4 paper.

② Place spoonfuls of the spinach in a grid at regular intervals on one sheet.

③ Top with the cubes of Brie and sprinkle with the nutmeg.

④ Brush the pasta around the edges and between the filling with a little water.

⑤ Place the second sheet of pasta over the top and press down between the mounds of filling and around the edges to seal.

⑥ Using a sharp knife, cut between the mounds to give squares. Check they are sealed.

⑦ Cook in a large pan of salted boiling water for about 8 minutes.

⑧ Drain and serve with the lemon juice squeezed over and seasoned to taste.

PASTA SETTING FOR THE PASTA
PLUS 20 MINUTES SHAPING AND COOKING

Index